FAISAL ALAJMI

Dogs in the Ancient Arabic Stories

Author's contacts, Email: faisalalalajmi1441@gmail.com. Instagram: faisalalalajmi1441

First edition

Translation by arapenz.com, translator: Jihad Elsaqa.

This book was professionally typeset on Reedsy.
Find out more at reedsy.com

Contents

Preface

For Arabs, The dog has a special status incomparable to any other animal. This is predictable as it is their companion in any place whether at home or on journeys. It is the guard of their homes and cattle. It protects not only their elderly but also the playgrounds of their children. It is described and well known as loyal. It is the perfect exemplar of loyalty.

Traditionally, at the golden ages, Arabs discussed everything including dogs. In fact, dogs had a significant share in the Arab cultural heritage. Some wrote complete books on dogs and some mentioned it in their books on animals. Dogs are always mentioned in stories and examples of loyalty.

In this book, I have collected as much as possible of stories on dogs in the ancient Arab cultural heritage. Unimaginable Stories of loyalty are collected here, and trusted scholars and writers told them all.

In writing this book, I was also motivated by the stories on dogs' loyalty we often here at present. For those two reasons, I embarked on this book.

I organized it into five chapters:

- Chapter 1: includes stories on dogs written by one of the greatest Arab writers, Al-Jahiz, (death date: 869 AD) in his famous Book on Animals.
- Chapter 2: tales, sayings, jokes, and poetry written by scholars and writers other than Al-Jahiz.
- Chapter 3: dogs in Arab proverbs as it were the center of many

proverbs as it was famous for loyalty.

- Chapter 4: dogs superiority to many of those who wear clothes by Ibn Al-Marzban (Death date: 921 AD).
- Chapter 5: Stories about dogs in the Arab heritage.

To illustrate the age of writing the stories, I include the death date of the writers. when the death date is not stated, the source of the story will be our reference. I state the death date of all writers. Some stories were written during the life of the writer of this book, while others were written decades and centuries before the writer was born.

I hope this collection is useful and I hope it achieves its purpose, which is to highlight the greatness of the Arab cultural heritage especially in the golden ages that started about fourteen and a half-century ago.

1

Dogs in the Book of Animals by Al-Jahiz

Al-Jahiz (died: 869 AD) is one of the greatest Arab writers in history. He has left humanity a great heritage. One of the most important Al- Jahiz's books is the Book of Animals. We will mention some of his writings on the dog. This book is a reference for all authors.

A Brief of the author and his book:

He is Amr Ibn Bahr Abu Usman, a top figure in literature, and the head of the Jahziyyah division of the Mu'tazilites.

He was born in Basra, where he also died. He suffered from Hemiplegia at the end of his life and died while a book was on his chest. He died when large books fell on him.

He has many books, including "Al-Bayan & Tabyeen," which is one of the four books considered the pillars of literature, as stated by the founder of sociology Ibn Khaldun (d. 1406 C.E). The remaining three books are "the writer's literature" by Ibn Qutaiba (d. 889 AD), "Al-Kamel" by Al Mubarrad (d. 899 C.E), and "the Book of Al-Nawader" by Abu Ali al-Qali (d. 967 AD) Baghdadi. Books other than these four are just branches and sequels.

Al- Jahiz called his book "The Animal" because it is built, as he says, on tracing evidence in the life on Allah's great wisdom and unique power.

This book is one of the greatest and biggest books. It is the first encyclopedia of its kind in the history of the Arabs, written by Al-Jahiz in old age and severe hemiplegia, after the killing of Mutawakkil in 861 C, E. He presented it to the Minister Mohammed bin Abdul Malik Zayat (d. 847 C.E), and included an extensive introduction about the art of writing and the secrets of authorship, including long chapters in defense of his books, including the book of animals. Therefore, in the art of writing and the history of the Arabic book, it is considered similar to the introduction of Ibn Khaldun in the science of history.

I have quoted what is written about dogs and ignored what does not benefit our subject. The book includes what was said about dogs from many different aspects and mentions the experience of his predecessors in the breeding of dogs and its pros and cons.

When I read about dogs, I found that a lot of writers quoted the words of Al-Jahiz. Therefore, I devoted to Al-Jahiz a special chapter, and another related chapter on the sayings of writers after him and what they added about dogs.

Here, we quote what was quoted about the dog, including an interesting dialogue about people who prefer the dog and those who prefer the cock. Al-Jahiz says: If I said: the dog and the cock have such a special status that two of the most prominent scholars, two elders from the top speakers, and prestigious thinkers, devoted time to mention their merits and equals and to compare between them.

An interesting talk, if I mentioned it incomplete, not a single book will be enough. I have mentioned a particular part of this interesting dialogue, and perhaps, if I will not get weakened, I will one day include this interesting dialogue in a separate book along with explanations and comments.

Al-Jahiz's writing about dogs:

(A dialogue on a dog)

I said: If a dog had the qualities of a wild animal, it would not accompany humans and avoid lions. it would not hate woods and take urban places as homes. It would not be afraid of wildlands and stay away from uninhabited areas. It would not love people's homes and places.

If a dog had the qualities of cattle, the attributes, shape, and food, it would not eat meat or attack people.

Yes, dogs jump at his owner and his family.

(A dialogue on the dog)

Abu Ishaq said: if a thief feeds it a piece of bread during the day, it will let him go and will turn around him at night.

In this aspect, it is a bribe and a corrupt; however, it has an ugly voice and its foolish attributes appear when it is awake or asleep. It sleeps all day on the same street, where people walk, in markets, at crossroads, and on the ways. It stays up late barking and making noise tiredly, furiously, and angrily. It runs around back and forth. It loves sleeping when needed. If another animal comes closer to it, it shows the worst panic and the most considerable cunning and becomes the most parking and noisy. If it is left alone peacefully without being approached by an animal or a human being, it does not also feel at peace because it always expects harm, which makes him on the ready all the time. If it is not left in peace, it becomes the worst creature on earth because it is the strongest panicked and the least patient. That's why it harms itself; the empty roads are open for it and the walls are there for it to rest.

Moreover, all creatures that contradict people's habits are hated. People sleep at night that Allah made it the rest time. People stay awake during the day because Allah made that time suitable for people to do all their activities.

The dog's owner said: if we said: dogs sleep during the day and wake up at night like kings; if the opposite were more appropriate, kings would do it.

What you have mentioned that dogs sleep on roads and considered it bad qualities that it sleeps on streets, inhabited ways, and in markets, is the dog's business as it knows what is the best for it.

The dog would not sleep in the market, if it does know that his sleep on empty roads would make him exposed to dangers, fools and boys who would harm his bones with their sticks and boards if they found him asleep away from men they fear or elders who have mercy and deter fools. It does not face these situations in markets.

However, guard's dogs are the one that often found in markets because it is where they live.

Therefore, it is a great mistake to compare an animal to humans. We know that all animals on earth are active at night because it is time for them to fine food and mate as they can see at night.

(Generosity of dogs)

The dog's owner said: cocks are not in any way similar to dogs. Some dogs have famous names and titles.

Its honors, attributes, triumphs, and breeds are kept in genealogical records, eternal registers, and counted birth books such as the dog, Gasan. Its name is Al-Sahlab bn Al Barak bn Yahia Bn Wathab bn Mozfr bn Maharesh.

(Evidence on dog's good attributes)

Some people who knew it said: the distance between a dog's hand and his legs is a sign of speed- provided that its back is short.

He said: they describe it as having a small head and a long thick neck.

It also should look coherent. Its ears are flat, and its anger is extreme. A long-distance should be between Its two ears. Its eyes should be blue; its eye-balls are tall; its pupil should be protruding; it has a long nose and wide jawbones; its forehead is wide and protruding. The hair under his mouth and on his cheeks should be thick and look like a ring. It has shorthands and long legs, which enables it to run up fast like a rabbit.

They said: dogs that can run up like a rabbit are the ones with short hands and long legs.

Its chest should be long and thick. The part of its chest that is closer to the ground should be broad. Its upper arm should be thick; its hands are straight; its fingers are fitted together during walking or running, which prevents the accumulation of dust or anything that would harm it. It should be smart and active and have a broad back. The distance between the joints of his bones should be long; the distance between the root bones of the thighs connected to the root of the tail should be long. The thighs should be thick, stiff and muscled. Its neck should be firm and its waist should be soft. The skin between the root of the thigh and chest should be long. Its legs should be straight. Its knees should have a curve and its legs should be short and as solid as wood.

It is not bad for females to have long tails, but it is bad for males. Also, soft hair indicates strength. This is favorable in all predatory animals including birds and four-legged. For feathered birds, soft feather is favorable.For hairy animals, a soft hair like the hair of horses is a good sign.

It was said: the dog should be extremely resistant to its chain. The bones after the two sides should be as small as three fingers.

It was said: the most definite sign of vigor is to have a claw on its legs, one of them, or its tale. It should be removed from the legs because it would prevent the dog from running.

(The best food for dogs)

The best food for dogs is dried bread soaked in water and some oil. This is like grass to horses; it makes it a strong runner.

It was said: the best food for nourishing a dog is a cooked head and haired feet without bones. If a dog eats butter, it should be three bowels twice or three times a day; this will help it gain weight. It is also said that this diet makes old dogs look and hunt like young ones. Bones and porridges are the worst food if you want the dog to be a runner.

(Medical treatment of a dog)

A piece of a fat tail mixed with sheep wool and cow butter is a portion of good nurturing food for a dog. It also cures abdominal ache and worms. It eliminates all worms and dirt in its belly.

The best treatment for injured paw pads is to apply the medicine for three days and to wrap the paw to prevent the dog from using it. Also, tar can be applied to its hands and legs.

It was said that Khozaima bn Tarkhan Al-Asady, who belonged to Hamzan, said: the best treatment for a dog is to give it an injection.

The philosopher (Aristotle) claimed that if a dog has worms in its abdomen, it should eat ears of wheat; it will be cured.

He claimed that when dogs get sick, they eat a certain type of grass so it is cured.

(Iyas bn Moawiya's insight)

It was said: when Iyas bn Moawiya went out, so he heard the bark of a dog. He said: this dog is firmly tied.

Then he heard its barking again, so he said: it is released now.

They went to the place where the water was and asked the people there who confirmed Iyas' saying.

Ghaylan Abu Marawan said: how did you know that the dog was tied and released?

He said: when a dog is tied, its bark is heard from one place. When it was released, its bark sounded at times far and sometimes near. This is the way.

It was said: Iyas bn Moawiya was passing by water at night when he heard a strange bark of a dog.

He was asked: how did you know it was strange?

He said: it sounded submissive and got firmly at the end.

They checked it and found that it was a strange dog tied and the other dogs were barking at it.

(Evidence on the significance of the dog)

A dog's owner said: the evidence of the significance of the dog is that people talk a lot about it when to mention its merits or evil. It is even mentioned in Quraan twice: once to give it credit and the other time is to dishonor it.

It is also mentioned in the sayings of the prophet, in poetry, tales, and derivatives. It is also mentioned in omens, fortunetelling, visions, and dreams. It is talked about in relation to jinn, predatory animals and cattle.

If you decided that it is evil and inferior or cunning and lowness based on what was said about it, you should know that the sayings about the merits of the dog is much more and its favorable traits are more famous.

Nothing combines as much as bad manners such as laziness because manners opposing laziness support attentiveness and create a good reputation for their owner.

Similarly, attributed related to laziness cannot be related to attentiveness. The same idea applied to the attributes pertaining to attentiveness;

they cannot co-exist with laziness because an attentive person is better than a lazy one.

(What a dog can do those humans cannot do?)

We will mention some of Allah's gifts to dogs that make them able to do things that you, the human, cannot do, in spite of your disrespect and injustice to it. This wisdom cannot be but sweet; these meanings cannot be but unique, and these feelings cannot be but soft. We know that if the person with the softest feeling, the most attentive mind, the most appropriate mentality, the perfect experience and knowledge compared the things that a dog can usually do to his own ability, he would realize that he is helpless and foolish and has limited abilities and inaccurate insight. What a human being does not know is that the world was not created based on his opinion, is not limited by his mind, realization, love or desire. The one who created the universe does not need a consultation, cooperation, support, help, experience or patience.

We will be stating some sentence; god's willing:

(The dog's experience in hunting)

You should know that a dog can, upon seeing deer, identify the sick and the healthy ones. It can also differentiate between a buck and a nanny. Upon seeing a heard, a dog targets the buck, although it knows that the buck is stronger and jumps a longer distance. It ignores nannies although they are less strong and jump a short distance. But, the dog knows that a buck would want to be after running for a short time.

(What happens to animals when panicked?)

All animals, when panicked, have either incontinence and dripping or urinary retention.

Also, animals whipped on the shoulder or beaten by a stick on buttocks suffer from the same issue. Many animals feel the need to pee or defecate.

Also, some hero knights drip when they see the enemy because of the terrifying situation.

When a male goat suffers from urine retention, it cannot pee in spite of the strong need to do it. Moreover, jumping, running, moving, and raising the legs together while running makes the male-goat unable to run fast and to jump long distances. It becomes breathless so it becomes easy for the dog to catch it.

Goat antelope does not retain urine when it panics. It gets rid of it gradually, similar to pregnant female camels that reject a male. This is because the path of the urine inside the body is wide and it can get out easily. Therefore, females can retain their speed for a longer time than males.

Only dogs know this by nature.

An experienced dog knows it by nature without difficulty. It does not need to learn, wait, or plan. It is its instincts that were given to it by the creator who created the brain, the thinker, the logical, the illness, the cure, the treatment and the curer. The creator organizes the universe for a reason in favor of all the creatures.

(The dog's skills in hunting tricks)

One thing about the dog, its owner takes it out to hunt even if it is snowy, and the land is covered by so many layers of ice that there becomes so much snow.

Moreover, the wind may blow at the ice, which makes it flat like a smooth stone or a glassy rock that no foot, mule, hoof or paw can stand firm on it without hard fixing or hard trying and keeping the two legs apart. The dog's owner takes it out. Although he is a sane person and an experienced hunter, he cannot determine the place of rabbit holes in the vast land or home of deer and foxes. The hunter cannot identify the place of the homes of any of the animals. A dog goes around forward, backward, right and left smelling and tracing until it reaches the holes where animals live. It tracks and evokes animals because of its breath. Breath and the vapor of their mouths and bodies, and the heat coming out from the bottom of the land make the snow on the holes melt. It becomes soft and breakable. Only a skillful hunting dog can do this. No hunter, shepherd, tracker, or farmer can do it.

A dog also is skillful in chasing animals that climb high mountains such as rabbits. It climbs up the hills carefully and cleverly and can reach animals that can never be found by the dog owners and falconers.

(The Instinctive attention of the dog)

A friend of mine told me that he locked his dog inside the house and closed the door at the time when his cock used to return from the market with meat. When he stroked a knife against another, the dog barked, got alerted, and tried to open the door because it thought that the cock had returned home from the market and was honing the knife to cut the meat.

He said: at night, we did the same to know if the dog can recognize the time, but it did not move!

He said: I did the same with another dog, and it lightly alerted. When the cock returned and honed the knife as I did, the dog tried to open the door!

He said, I thought: it seems that the dog can recognize the time, so it got alerted, and when it did not smell meat, it knew that it was not necessary. Then, when it heard the sound of a knife when the time had not oases, and it smelt meat in the kitchen, it was evoked to bark. Also, it could differentiate between the way I hone the knife and the way the cock did it. In either case, it is fascinating.

When the meat is just two or three arms-length away from me, I cannot smell it. Only when I get it closer to my nose, I can recognize its smell. This is really strange.

There was a time when people of a road between Astfanous, the house of a servant and vendors of Bani Manker's square complained about a dog that lied on the road and never crossed the guard during the week except on Fridays when it moved from its place to the house of the servant before the afternoon prayer. It stayed there as long as there was meat hanging at the butcher's.

The servant always got sheep slaughtered at the butcher's only on Fridays; therefore, the dog used to go to her house on Friday. No one ever saw it approaching the house on other days. It waited until it was Friday afternoon to go to her. This cannot be done unless the dog could tell the time.

Many people have regular activities on Fridays such as praying or place to go and they sometimes forget and are reminded by other people. This dog never forgot and never needed a reminder. All the people in this story confirmed that when they realized its habit, they paid attention to it and fond it never changed this habit.

(A story on the dog's loyalty)

Abu Al-Hassan bin Khalawi narrated Abu Obeida's narration of poetry:

His neighbor and brother run away from him... His dog that he has beaten searches for him

Abu Obeida said: this was said when a man went to desert to wait for something to ride, a dog that he owned followed him. He beat and shunned the dog as he hated to be followed by it. He also threw a rock at the dog, which refused to go away.

When he arrived at the place where he should wait, the dog stayed close to him. At this time, some of the man's enemies came to him to revenge. His neighbor and brother were with the man but they left him alone and ran away. The attackers came closer to the man and threw him in a shallow well. They added dust to the well until his head was completely covered, and they flattened the land over him. The dog was barking and growling. When they left, the dog cam close to the well and kept barking and digging using its hand until the man's head was revealed. He could now breathe and was rescued; otherwise, he would have died and decomposed.

Meanwhile, some people passed by and was surprised by the dog's act. They thought it was digging a grave. They looked and saw the man there. They took him out alive and carried him to his home. It was said that this well was called the dog's well, and it was located on the right of Al-Najaf.

This story indicates that the dog is loyal by nature and has instinctive friendliness and extreme protectiveness. It is wise and patient. It is also characterized by generosity and a sense of gratitude. It is beneficial and helpful. What the dog did was clear from any form of pretending or affectation.

(The reason why a loin requests dogs)

Some merchants claimed something that I cannot know the reason for it. They said that they are sure that lions prefer dogs because they envy them and not because they love their meat.

They said that when a lion approaches water surfaces and rivers, they eat crabs, frogs, tortoises, and turtles. In fact, the lion is too gourmand to be selective regarding meat.

They said: the lion is so because when it targets the strayed donkeys, sheep, or animals near a village, the dog barks strongly, and the people get alerted and fight the lion. They protect their properties and fight the lion so it returns empty-handed.

That's why the lion starts by the dog to prevent it from alarming the people. Then, it attacks the whole village. Therefore, lions prefer eating dogs.

(The dog's weapon and the cock's weapon)

They said: a cock is not of the same kind of a dog because when a dog attacks a cock, the latter will be completely destroyed.

The dog's weapon, which is in his mouth, is stronger than the cock's spur in its leg. Its sound is clearer, reaches a longer distance, and his eyes are more attentive.

(Defense of the dog)

The dog depends on itself and protects others. It takes care of its family so it is very supportive and not costly for its owner.

The number of cattle that run from their owners, disobey them, butt them, or kill their family in one day is more than the number of dogs doing so in one year.

When a bellwether butts, it is slaughtered without agitation or being trifled with.

A workhorse bites and runs without being agitated or trifled.

Contrary to these animals, dogs do not bite anyone unless they are extremely agitated; Also, they bark and threaten more than they bite.

(A dog can identify his owner and is happy upon seeing him)

A dog can differentiate between his owner, his slave, his handmaid, and guests. Even if the owner of the house traveled away for a year, the dog would be happy upon seeing him, will wag his tail and bark in joy. It expresses deep and incomparable yearning.

(Another story about the dog's loyalty)

A friend of mine told me: we had a puppy, and I had a servant who loved it so much and was passionate about taking care of it and supporting him. He traveled away from Al Basra for months. I said to my friends: do you think the dog will remember the face of the absent servant after leaving it when it was puppy; The dog is a grownup now that raises its leg to pee?

They said: we do not doubt that it forgot everything about him, even his face.

He said: while I was at home, I heard its bark from behind the house door. I did not feel that its bark is for blaming, scolding, or threatening. I saw that it was wagging its tail in joy and excitement.

Shortly, I saw the servant arrives. The dog went around his legs and stood at his thighs. It looked at his face and barked in happiness.

It was so happy that I thought it was ill. Afterward, the servant used to travel for two or three months. He sometimes comes to Baghdad then returns to the army after a few days. I always knew that the servant was coming from the dog's wagging tail and barking.

I said to my family: the servant must have arrived and is going inside now along with the dog.

I was told that maybe this puppy until it became an adult dog, was provided by some food to eat as much as it can; then, the rest is kept away. Maybe the thing is given to the dog when it is full so it tests it and the rest of the food that was kept away is made available to it to eat when it feels hungry.

(The discipline of a dog)

Some boys and some of the people of a neighborhood claimed that there was a dog that barked at all riders entering the neighborhood until it reaches touches the hock of the workhorse. It barked at anyone whether he was a stableman or the owner of the animal. However, when the dog saw Mohamed Bn Abdul-Malak entering or leaving from the gate of the neighborhood, it never barked at him or at his animal. It never blocked his way. The dog used to go inside the passageway quickly.

I asked about it, so I was told that when the dog barked, the servant shouted at it and beat it until it went inside the passageway. This happened three times until the dog got used to going inside the passageway on its own upon seeing Mohamed bn Abdul Malak. Then, when he left, the dog started jumping at the hocks of the animals of Al-Shakirya.

I found that it was a famous story there.

He said: also, when it came close while we were having lunch, we rebuked it once or twice. Then, it never came close to the place where we rebuked it. It also did not go away from the place because of its greed. If we threw something to it, it ate it and came a bit close to it.

We used to trick it by throwing a piece of bread an arm-length away from its pen. When they ate it, it became greedy and came close to the buffet and in this way, it passed its limits.

We wanted to test the dog to talk about later, but feeing a dog and cats from the buffet is wrong for many reasons:

First, it will get used to it to the extent that it will sometimes try to reach its hand to the food on the table or eat by its mouth. Also, it may vomit what it has eaten while being seen. Perhaps, it did not want to be seen, so it does not vomit.

A chief or the house owner should not see such things contrary to the servants.

(In defense of the dog)

Regarding what they say about the dog's meanness and dishonesty, they say that when a thief wants to enter a house, he feeds the dog guarding the house many times day and night. He also gets closer to the dog and pats its back until he becomes familiar with the dog. When he comes at night, the dog will leave the house and its contents to him. However, this belief is a result of misjudgment, which makes people see wrong as right.

It is unfair to the dog and is challenging for the people who defend the dog. Significantly, although this is used as an accusation to the dog, it is, in fact, evidence that a dog deserves praising. The excessive friendliness and gratitude of the dog prevent it from attacking the thief because of his kindness to it; it is similar to people with extreme modesty as they are described as weak. Similarly, people with excessive generosity are described as careless. Also, sometimes, a prudent man is somehow inattentive, which increases the man's forgiveness. Extreme prudence may prevent many good things if the person is not forgiving.

You, the arguer, you say that, because of the kindness and generosity of the thief to it, the dog is grateful and avoids harming the person who is kind to him in fear of being unthankful. This is, in fact, a positive opinion and a great privilege.

If the dog could know the consequences and events; if it could differentiate between things that are urgent or not; if it knew the sources and resources of thing; if it could choose the worst and best; if it could verify things, fear shame, ask for or give evidence; if it could differentiate between evidence and suspicion, guaranteed and doubtful things; if it could verify drawbacks; if it feared from air deflection and natural changes, it would be among the most significant legally competent and the top tested.

(The self-glory of the dog)

They said: moreover, a dog does not agree to sleep or lie on dirty or muddy sides of the streets. It sits down on the back of the carpets and is not satisfied with carpets. It sits on cushions and does not stay at a place without its companion.

It is so noble that it always chooses the classiest spot to sit down in the place where the host left it to stay safe and protected. It always chooses the place on the top front; a dog does not hesitate to climb up to lie there.

Among the reasons why Moawyia used to have a cabin after Al-Bark attacked him with a sword, was that he saw a dog on a platform. This is how a well-dressed man is welcomed without letting a dog bark at him when he approaches the house.

A dog is very arrogant and proud; it has a strong sense of self-glory, uniqueness, and vanity. This is evident by the fact that when a dog barks at a man at night and there is no guard to prevent it and the man cannot run, the only solution for a man is to sit surrendering in front of the dog.

When the dog sees him this way, it comes closer to him, let him go without attacking him. It is as if when it felt in control when it sees the man submissive to him, it prefers to make him feel humiliated. It is similar to the act of Arabs who used to cut the forelocks of the captivated knights after deciding to let them go and bestow favor upon them.

If the Arab refused to cut his forelock, the captor would condemn him in everlasting poetry and prose that would be more harmful to him than cutting his firelock. Although the captive might not go home until his forelock grew again, the feeling of humiliation caused by the haircut would be noticed in his face and kept in his heart.

(An opinion of the dog)

It was said that Motraf Ibn Abdullah hated that someone yelled at a dog or rebuked it in any way. When he invoked Allah's curse upon the dog's owners who did not prevent it from entering his praying place, he said:

May Allah prevent them from the yields of its hunt! This indicates that he had a good opinion of dogs.

It was said: Jesus, the son of Maryam, peace be upon him, was passing by disciples with a dog carcass.

Some of them said: What a strong rotten smell it has!

He said: you'd better say: what white teeth it has!

It was said: once a man said to a dog: go away, Woe to you! Hammam Ibn Al-Hareth said: Woe is to people of Hell.

(The son of woof woof)

There was a man whose name was "Kalb," which means a dog in Arabic. His son was playing on the street.

A man asked him: who are your father?

The boy said: Woof, Woof!

(The nobility of dogs)

It was said: a man brought his friend before Al-Moghera to judge a dispute between them. The friend intimidated the man by his friendship with Al-Moghera, so the man told so to Al-Moghera, saying: he threatened me by his friendship with you and claimed that you would give him a favor because of that.

Al-Moghera said: yes, friendship counts. Even a rapacious dog gives favor because of friendship.

If a rapacious dog does so, what do you think of people? Also, you become keen on not harming a person who cherishes friendship even if he is among a thousand people.

All dogs are characterized by such nobility.

A dog protects its owner and his women, whether present or absent, attentive or inattentive, asleep or awake. It is never neglectful in this regard even they maltreat it; it never forsakes them, even if they abandoned it.

(The dog's sleep)

At the sleeping time, a dog's eyes are the most alerted compared to all animals. A dog sleeps during the day as they are not needed for guarding. It sleeps infrequently and scarcely.

It is in its deepest sleep while its eyes open enough to guard; it stays in this state for only one hour. However, it is always more attentive than a wolf; its hearing ability is stronger than a horse; it is more cautious than a magpie; moreover, it has a long-distant sound.

(A dog treats itself)

A dog is rarely bored and extremely patient about disaffection. It can endure severe injuries and deep stab and arrow wounds. If it is wounded, it keeps cleaning the wound with its saliva until it is cured. A dog knows that its saliva is its cure. It does not need a doctor, ointment, or treatment.

(In the dog's defense)

A defender of dogs said: if you searched among all Bedouin people around the globe for a tent whose people do not have at least one dog, you would not find any. This was the norm in the pre-Islamic epoch and it is still the same even after embracing Islam.

Abu-Abad Al-Nomeri said: buildings are only considered a village if there are a barking dog and a crowing rooster.

When Ahmed bn Al-kharky said: a village becomes a real village only it includes a tailor and a teacher, Abu Abad said: crazy if so, it becomes a city.

A dog touches the face of its owner to look at his eyes and face. It loves its owner and stays close to him. It plays with him and his kids through soft and non-painful biting, although its grinders are so strong that they can crack rocks, and its fangs are so sharp that is can break stones.

You see what it can do to the compact bones and hard vertebras that are neither old and decayed nor fresh and have the fat that makes it chewable and soft. You see how a dog can break and smash it. Then, if it is somehow too hard for the dog to chew it, it swallows the bones when feeling hungry, knowing for sure that it will be processed, digested, and dissolved.

A dog makes many types of sounds and melodies; it moans, sings, chants, groans, bawls, growls, barks, wags, and makes a special sound when happy. It also makes a sound similar to wailing when getting ready for hunting. Moreover, it makes a sound between barking and wailing while playing with others of its kind in summer's early mornings. A dog takes careful steps on pebbles; for example, it adjusted its steps when walking on pebbles on flat ground. In fact, a dog's steps depend heavily on its weight.

When passing by a sold water-surfaced valley, the dog avoids the babbling spots underneath.

(when the wolf attacks sheep in the morning)

It is said that a wolf usually attacks sheep in the morning because it watches the dog and knows that dogs are inactive in the morning because it stays up late to guarding.

(The cause of revelation of a verse about dog hunting)

When the Prophet (peace be upon him) told Zayd "horses are goodness" and called him Zayd the goodness, Zayd had not asked something from him or asked for a favor, but he said: prophet of Allah, there are two men among us one of them is called Zreh and the other called Aba Dagana. They have five dogs that hunt deer, what do you think about their hunting?

Allah revealed this verse:

(They ask thee what is lawful to them (as food). Say: lawful unto you are (all) things good and pure: and what ye have taught your trained hunting animals (to catch) in the manner directed to you by Allah: eat what they catch for you, but pronounce the name of Allah over it).

The first thing that makes you think highly of dogs is that the gentle person who asked the prophet and got a unique title asked only about the dog.

Secondly, most significantly, Allah revealed these verses upon this occasion: (lawful unto you are (all) things good and pure) so its hunt is called good and pure. Moreover, the verse says (what ye have taught your trained hunting animals (to catch)). This is evidence that dogs can be taught and trained. Also, the verse says (in the manner directed to you by Allah). If Allah did not accept teaching and training dogs, he would not attribute it to Himself. Then, the verse says: eat what they catch for you, but pronounce the name of Allah over it.

The first thing that makes a dog great is that it catches the prey for the hunter. People who advocate hunting say: hunters catch their prey for themselves except dogs; they catch it for their owners.

If we consider the prophet's saying to Zayd is Sunnah, mentioning the dog in the verse is even more revered because Quraan outweighs Sunnah.

Hesham reported that Ibn Abbas gave names to Zareh's dogs and Abi-Degana's dogs as follows:

Al-Mokhtales, Ghalab, Al-Quneis, Salhab, Sarhan, and Al-Mota'tes.

(Knowing whether the dog is young or old)

A dog's owner said: the age of a dog is known from its teeth. If the dog's teeth are black, it means the dog is old. If its teeth are sharp and white, it means it is young. He said: a male dog has more teeth.

(A dog's sharp sight)

Kotrob, Mohamed Bin Al-Mostaneer Al-Nahawi, once said: "I swear to Allah that a guy has a sharper sight than a dog, a sharper sense of hearing than a dog, and a stronger sense of smell than a dog."

(The best horse)

A dog's owner said: Mohamed Ibn Sallam reported Saeed Ibn Sakhr's words saying: Moslem Ibn Amr sent a cousing to Al-Sham and Egypt to buy a horse for him.

He said: I do not know about horses- she owned dogs.

He replied: do not you have a dog?

He said: yes

He replied: search for the horse that has the best qualities of dogs.

So he brought a horse that no Arab had alike.

(The dog's frightfulness)

Once I went out in the foredawn in order to have a talk. When I reached the square of the neighborhood, few dogs approached me irritated. They were big and the type typical for guarding.

While I was avoiding them as they came closer, they suddenly became silent. Then each one of them hid in a corner as if terrified and hiding. I heard a human voice, so I seized the chance that they stopped barking. I thought: there must be a reason. At this moment, two men approached with a thick-haired gigantic dog wearing a collar; I have never seen a dog bigger than this one.

I said: they stooped barking and hid because they feared it, although dogs do no have a leader.

This chapter included part of the great writer Al-Jahiz in his valuable book, the Animal, which became an essential reference for many researchers in the past and present.

2

News and sayings

Al-Jahiz's book is so comprehensible that he did not leave much for others to discuss further. His book has become a reference for writers, and many of them quoted him. However, some authors mentioned benefits that are not discussed by Al-Jahiz, which I present in this chapter. Here, we quote some statements of scholars, writers, poets, and geographers about dogs, in addition to what was reported about them.

Al-Abshihi (d. 1448) says of the types and ages of dogs:

It is known that dogs come in two types: Ahli and Saluki; these two types are similar. However, the female of a Saluki dog is a faster learner than the male. This animal is patient and fit. It also honors prestigious people.

It is a kind of animal that is grateful. It was said that the female gives birth to twelve puppies at the maximum rare case. More often, it gives birth to five or six, and perhaps one. Usually, The dog lives ten years, and it perhaps reaches twenty years.

Ibn 'Abd al-Hadi (d. 1503) says of the nature of the dog:

The nature of the Saluki is that if the antelope is close or far away, it can differentiate between the male and female, although they have the same walk.

It can also differentiate between a dead person and a person who is playing dead. Therefore, the Romans do not bury their dead until they are exposed to dogs, as upon sniffing, the dog gives a sign to indicate that the person is alive or dead. It is said: This is only in some kind of dog called Alaltti, with a small body and short legs; it is also called the Chinese.

The females of the Saluki are faster learners than males, and the cheetah is the opposite.

Al-Zamakhshari (d. 1144 AD) says of the wits of dogs:

The fox knows that playing dead may be believed by the hunter but not by dogs. If it feels a hunter is coming, the fox lies down and inflates its waist so that the hunter does not suspect its death and walks away.

If it feels a dog is coming, the fox runs like the wind, because the dog can differentiate between those who are dead and those who are playing dead. Therefore, Zoroastrians do not place the dead in the coffin until a dog comes close to the body to confirm that the person is dead.

The dog may play dead. Some said: I saw a weak puppy hit and knocked by boys, so it stretched like the dead. Although they kicked it, the puppy did not move until they were sure it was dead so they left it alone.

Then, I looked and saw it opening its eyes looking then bounced and fled.

The earth may have been covered with ice and snow. The experienced dog owner does not know where the beast is, the dog keeps looking and sniffing until it stands at the hole and provokes animals inside.

Ibn Qutaiba al-Dinuri (d. 889 AD) says of the purest mouth and best swimmer animal:

It is said: No predator has a mouth purer than a dog's, nor a beast has a purer mouth than the antelope's. It is said: No animal has a mouth more stinky than a lion's and a falcon's. No predator is better at swimming than a dog.

Ibn al-Jawzi (d. 1201 AD) says in his book, *Akhbar Al-Azkiya*, about a dog with the people of the house:

One of the features and actions of animals that indicate their prudence is that birds live in inhabited houses only, and if abandoned by people, birds leave also.

As for cats, they stay in the house, even if its people left.

a dog departs with the people of the house and does not turn to the house.

A Sheikh's dog attacks his students

One interesting story was that the Imam al-'Amash (may Allah have mercy on him) (deceased: 765 AD) one of the greatest scholars of his time was a bit strict with the students. He expelled them by any means, such as unleashing his dog at them.

"We used to come to Al-A'amash, and he has a dog that hurt people of Al-Hadith," Jarir, one of his students, said.

He said: We came to him one day and it was dead, so we gathered at him.

When he saw us, he wept and said: the one, who ordered the good and forbid evil, perished," he meant the dog.

It was strange that his students did not get bored.

But do not be surprised because they lived during the peak of the Arab golden ages, and his students were the prominent scholars of that time.

The Number of dog names

It was narrated that the writer Abu Bakr al-Khwarizmi (deceased: 993 AD) entered the Council of Al-Saheb ibn Abbad (deceased: 995 AD) wearing worn clothes. The council was full of nobles and poets from many countries from all over the globe. He went up the pavilion, so the attendees belittled him, and one of them said, thinking that he does not know Arabic: Who is this dog?

Abu Bakr al-Khwarizmi said: The dog is the one who does not know twenty languages in the dog. The attendees became silent and acknowledged the credit to him so he mentioned the names of the dog.

The story is repeated with Al-Maari:

Abu Al-Alaa Al-Maari (deceased: 1057 AD) entered one day to Al-Sharif Al-Murtada (deceased: 1044 AD) and found a man, the man said to him: Who is this dog?

Abu Al-Alaa said: the dog is the one who does not know seventy names of the dog.

When Al-Murtada got him near to test him and he was found knowledgable.

Imam Al-Suyuti (deceased: 1505 m) is the owner of the classifications and a rajaz poem titled: Al-Tabari Min Maarat Al-Maari.

He stated dog names. He says in the introduction: I have traced the language and I found and organized more than sixty names.

Why do they give their children names of dogs and predators?

Al-Dumairi (d. 1405 AD) says in his book The Animal's Great Life:

The Arabs do not find it embarrassing to give their children names or nicknames of dogs.

The word, Kelab in Arabic, which means dogs might be derived from the source, Mokalaba, which means jumping to attack. For example, I jumped attacking the enemy. Also, it might be the plural of kalb, dog, and it was called so to reflect their great number similar to calling lion, Asbaa, which literally means sevens or calling tigers Anmar, which literally means numbers.

It was said to Abu al-Duqish al-A'rabi: why do you give your sons bad names such asKalb, a dog, or Zeab, a wolf? And you give you servants the best names such as Marzouk and Rabah?

He said: the names of our children are chosen considering our enemies while the names of slaves are chosen considering us as if they intended optimism by doing so because Kalb, dog in English, comes from Mokalaba which means attacking the enemy.Kalba is the female of Kalb and its plural is kalbat without a short /i/.

One of the interesting stories is the story of Asmaa, the daughter of Roem and the wife of Wabra Bin Taghlab.

She was a wise, prudent literary woman who had many children (she lived around the third century AD).

She gave her children names of predator animals.

It was said: Wael bin Qasit passed and saw her alone in her tent, so he was about to attack her.

She said: I swear to God, if you attack me, I will try my predators.

He said: I see only you in the valley.

And she shouted to her sons: O Dog, O Wolf, O Cheetah, O Bear, O Sirhan, O Lion, O Hyena, O Tiger.

They came running with swords.

Wael said: This is the valley of lions.

The valley had this name ever since.

And they said to her: What is wrong?

She said: she came to us as a guest, and I loved to honor specially.

He left wondering about her offspring and her ready wits to think about an excuse to say to her children.

(Dearer than Kolaib)

One of the most famous people who were given a name of a dog was Kolaib Bin Rabia (deceased: 492 m), who was an exemplar of honor: there is a famous Arabian saying: (more honorable than Kolaib Bin Rabia). He was the chief of Rabia tribe at his time. When people came for water, they got it only upon his approval. Even when rain fell, people were allowed to get water from rain basins only after Kolaib got enough of it. When he said, " I have prohibited hunting of something," no one hunted it.

One of the habits of the Arabs before Islam was that when an honorable man settled in fertile land, he took a dog as a companion to accompany him when being over mountains or far away from his place. The dog would protect him by its bark that frightened whatever heard it; thus, the man would be protected from all directions.

Two of the most famous Arab tribes are Kalb bin Wabra and Kolab Bin Rabia.

Among the famous people who were nicknamed as "Kalb" (means a dog)

A'ed AlKalb (a dog visitor):

His name was Abdullah Ibn Musab al-Zubayri, who was the governor of a city for Rashid (d. 809 AD). He was nicknamed Al-Kalb because of his saying:

When I fell ill, no one of you visited me ... although when a dog of yours gets sick, I visit thee

And your disaffection is more painful than my illness..the disaffection of whom I love is grimness

His sons are now called " the sons of A'ed Al-Kalb "

A Dog Lover:

Ibn Hajar al-Asqalani (d. 1449) said that he was titled Abraham the Bazaar.

I do not know why he was called so, but perhaps because he loved dogs more than others. He was called a lover.

Amr Ibn Al-Aglan was named "Za Al-Kalb" (a dog's owner) because a dog always accompanied him.

Abu Ubaida said: He did not have a dog, but he went out invading with a dog that he accompanied during hunting. His companions said to him, the dog owner. And he was called so ever since. Some people called him, Amr al-kalb.

Samani (died: 1167 AD) said, about the title of Kalabzi, "This title is related to keeping and breeding dogs and hunting with them.

Breastfed by a bitch!

The mother of the most famous Arab poet, Amru al-Qays (d. 545 AD), nicknamed the Dalel King, died when he was a child, so his family fed him with milk of a bitch. His sweat smelled like dogs so women hated him.

Poetry about dogs: -

Imam Shafi'i (d. 820 AD) said:

(I wish my neighbors were dogs ... I wish I did not meet any human beings)

(Dogs rest in their pens ... and people's evil never rests)

(Save yourself and enjoy your loneliness ... you are happy when you are alone)

Hatem al-Ta'i (d. 578 AD), who is still an exemplar of generosity. Although he died fifteen centuries ago, Arabs still remember his generosity.

One day he was seen beating his son because he saw him hitting a dog that guided his guests to him. He said

I say to my son, whose hands beat ... a dog that he kept beating it

Take care of this dog... I am grateful to it

She guides my guests to me at night ... If the fire is faded

From the jokes of the memory of Zamakhshari (deceased: 1144 AD):

A man was told: why does a dog raise a leg while it is peeing?

He said: to not get its clothes dirty.

It was said: does a dog wear clothes?

He said: it imagines that it has clothes.

Abu Hayyan Al-Tawhidi mentioned another joke (deceased: about 1010 AD), he said: a drunken person came out and walked in the road so he fell and slept, and a dog came and licked his mouth and lips. The drunken Said: may your sons serve you and never lose you. Then, the dog lifted his leg and peed on his face, so he said: and hot water? God bless you.

Al-Tartushi (d. 1126 AD) said of the difference between wild and urban dogs:

The urban dog barks at guests push visitors back and shun requesters, while a wild dog supports its companion, informs about guests, and prevents thieves.

Dogs called by their names!

A man gave a dog to a son of Ibn Jamee (d. 808 AD).

He said: What is its name?

He said: "I do not know." he took out a notebook in which names of dogs were written, so he called it by all the names until it answered.

Dogs were also described in well-organized prose:

Abu Ishaq Al-Sabi (d. 994 AD) described dogs in a direct message: all dogs we have are of a noble race, significant gains, sweet graces, smart features, a sharp sight, relaxed ears, soft cheeks, slender sides, a broad chest, and a solid back. They are also honorable and robust runners. They do not touch the ground except slightly without excessiveness (because of its speed and lightness) and steps on it very lightly.

Moreover, dogs have a share of some famous places' names: -

Nagd Al-Kalba:

The reason for this name is that Malik bin Fahm al-Azdi (deceased: about 157 AD), had a neighbor who had a dog. When his nephews, Amr Ibn Fahim Ibn Ghanem, were passing by that man with their sheep, the dog barked at them and dispersed their sheep. One of them threw an arrow at it and killed it.

Malik's neighbor complained to him about what his nephews did. However, his nephews were more than his sons, so he could not do anything to them. He got angry and said: I swear to God that I will not live in a country where this happens to my guests. He walked until Amman, where he settled and the place where he traveled to was called Nagd Al Kalba ever since.

Suluq:

A city in the land of Yemen; Ibn al-Haik (died: 945 AD) said, "It was a great city and had great remaining monuments."

It has predatory dogs because they and wolves mate, so Suluqi dogs are born, which are the fiercest dogs.

The greatest Arab geographer, Yaqout al-Hamwi (d. 1229 AD) mentioned in his book, *Mogem AlBoldan, (The Dictionary of Countries)*, some cities named after dogs, including the following:

Al-Kalb:

A river named "Al-Kalb" (the dog) lies between Beirut and Sidon, which is one of the capitals in Al-Sham.

Al-Kalb (The dog): a place between Qoms and Al-Rai, one of the houses ofHaji Khorasan where they stay at the beginning of Ramadan.

Al-Kalb (the dog): a mountain that is one-day far from Yamamah. It is the mountain where Zarqa Al-Yamamah saw the vanguard of Taba.

Kalba (bitch): it is utter as the name of a female dog; Kalba is a place in Eram. Kalba is located in the suburbs of Oman on the sea coast.

Ibn al-Faqih (d. 951 AD), in his book Al-Baladan, told about dogs fighting lions:

The people of Nubia are singled out for the skill of shooting and the unique wonders of their country.

They have wonderful horses and camels that precede horses. They have dogs that fight lions.

Strange incident

In 1321, there was a strange incident chronicled by famous historians, headed by Ibn al-Wardi (d. 1349 AD), Taqi al-Din al-Maqrizi (d. 1441 AD), and Jalal al-Din al-Suyuti (d. 1505 AD), in which a dog in Cairo gave birth to thirty puppies. It was brought to the Sultan, who was surprised and asked astrologers about it but they did not know anything about it.

This is strange, no doubt. I did not report about similar incidents, but I keep it for myself because of my love of strange things and wonders since I was a child.

But I read a statement that changed me and made me excited to publish such news: "if this news is true, it is fantastic. If it is not true, we consider it from literature." this is the saying of the greatest Abbasid Khalifa, Harun al-Rashid (deceased: 809 AD). He said it when he heard Abi Al-Seri Sahl Al-Khazraji, who claimed that he was breastfed by the jinn and lived with him until he knew their wisdom, genealogy and poems! Harun wondered and said to him: (If you saw what you mentioned, you saw a wonder, and if you did not see it, you have written literature!).

3

Proverbs about dogs

Ibn Hamdoun (died: 1167 AD) says: Arabs described the dog, the caller of any stranger, the guider of any exotic person, the caller of generosity, the complement of blessings, causer of remembering his owner for the guests it brings by its barking.

Exotic person means the exotic guest; the person who is caused to be not present by the country. When it was very cold, the wind blew, and the fire was not still glowing, they spread the dogs around the district, made a shadow for them, and got them bounded to be wild so that they bark to guide the lost people.

Here are the famous proverbs mentioned by Abou Helal El Askary (died: after 1005 AD):

(Dog owners do not stay alone)

If the house owner leaves, he is not followed by a horse, a mule, a cock, a chicken, a pigeon, a cat, a sheep, a bird nor any pet living with people except the dog as it follows him wherever he goes, protects him and prefers him to its home and home town.

(Dog owners are always thanked)

The author of the proverb said: the dog is characterized by loving, obeying, protecting, and tracking who treats it well glibly, and it can differentiate his urine by smelling it. It obeys anyone it knows by satisfying, looking at and laughing in front of him.

(Dogs love who is moving a lot)

They are like men who love people and cannot stay in one place. If the dog owner is moving a lot, it becomes cheerful and follows him.

(Dogs cannot be forced to work)

They are like men who are not dedicated to any work they are forced to do.

Persians say that if the dog is forced to hunting, it will not satisfy its owner.

(Dogs see well)

All dogs see at nighttime as in daytime, and I do not know why this feature specializes dogs.

(Dogs are the greediest)

The greediness is the eagerness and glutton, and this feature characterizes all dogs. They eat quickly as if it is attracted to something.

(The courageous person is respectful)

It means that people seek protection with who is known by his courage as they respect him and fear from him, said by El Zobriqan Bin Badr (deceased : about 665 AD):

(Wolves attack who does not have dogs...and they stay away from any place protected by dogs)

It means the dog entering its tail between its legs, and it is applied to any man who wears a wrapper and puts its end between his legs and sticks it in his hips.

(Active dog is better than a lazy lion)

It is said that the weak professional active man is more beneficial for himself and his family than the strong lazy man.

Active means keep watching and watching at night and a man is guarding like servants are derived from it

(Easier than barking at clouds)

The dog in the desert spends the night under the clouds, and if it rains and the dog is exhausted, it is still barking at all clouds watched by it, and it is perhaps barking at the moon as the moon seems like a piece of the cloud if it appears from the east.

(When I asked for good, evil comes to me)

Man says it is asking for good; then, evil comes to him.

It said that: its origin is that a man staying in wasteland barked at dogs to bark at him if they are near to know the place of any person, but the wolves heard his voice and came to attack him.

Then, he said: When I asked for good, evil comes to me

Here are the proverbs of dogs mentioned by Abou Mansour El Thaaleby (deceased : 1038 AD)

(Tossom's Dog)

It is said when someone does good and rewarded by abuse

Tossom had a dog treated well by it, and then the dog guided the enemy to their place by its barking. Then, Tossom was attacked and killed by their enemy.

And Barakesh, a dog owned by a group of Arab escaped from its enemy accompanying Barakesh, guided the enemy, and then the enemy tracked them by Barakesh barking, attacked, and destroyed them. Therefore, they said Barakesh guided its owners as a proverb.

(Homal's Dog)

It is said as hungrier than Homal's dog.

Homal is a lady from the Arab. She kept a watchdog, let it hungry, and expelled it in the daytime. One night, it saw the moon, and then it barked at it as it thinks that it is a loaf because it is round. And after it feels so exhausted, it ate its tail as it was starving.

(Dog wool)

It said in distress and hardness

And it is said: the brain of the small ants, milk of bird, and it is said that he needed wool by shearing his dog, as the poet said:

(Who shears a dog for its wool... becomes, by your life, in need of wool)

(Dog stinginess)

It is said as an exemplary for the stingy.

Because if the dog obtains anything, it will not let someone eat from it. If someone wants to grab something from its hand, it will attack him.

(Dog care)

Arabs say that someone is more careful than dogs.

His morals are dog guarding, dog protection and dog gregariousness.

And it is said that the dog is more gregarious than the cat because the dog gets accustomed by man while the cat gets accustomed by the place.

(Dog killer)

He is Masama Bin Senan Abu Malik (deceased : 692 AD)

This calls him as he resorted to Ridda Wars to a group of the sons of Abdul Qais, and their dog was barking at him. He feared to be guided

He was afraid of the dog to guide for his place and killed it and then he was killed for killing it.

Malik Bin Masama was called the son of the dog killer.

(Let your dog hungry to follow you)

It was said for the first time by one of the Himyarite kings who oppressed his dependents and usurped their money. His wife forbade him saying: I fear that they become beasts after they were followers.

Then, he said to her: let your dog hungry to follow you. He has a brother who was demanded by the dependents to be the successor of the king. Then, they killed the kings, and his brother became his successor by them.

Then, Amer Bin Gozaima passed at him when he was dead and said: the dog can eat his master if he lets him hungry, and it becomes a proverb.

It is narrated that Abu Gaafar El Mansour (deceased : 775 AD) said once to his leaders: the Bedouin was true when he said, let your dog hungry to follow you.

One of them said to him: Hey, Prince of the Believers, I am afraid that if you do that, another one attracts it by a loaf, and then it follows him and leaves you.

El Mansour did not find any answer.

Here is one of the Arab examples mentioned by El Maidany (deceased : 1124 AD):

(Sleepier than the leopard)

Because the leopard is the sleepiest creature, and his sleep is not like the dog sleep, as the dog dozes while the leopard sleeps deeply. As well as, the leopard is heavier than the dog as the leopard can destroy any animal.

A lady from the Arabs said: my husband eats what he finds, whether leopard or lion and does not ask for what he is accustomed to.

(Dog beat wolf)

Ekrema said it (deceased : 723 AD), the lord of Bin Abbas (may Allah be pleased with them)

When he was asked about a man who usurped money from another man, and the usurped one was able to usurp his money, Does he usurp like what was usurped from him? Ekrema said: the dog beat the wolf to take from him what he took from him before.

It is said when the oppressor is defeated.

It was also said:

(A dog barking for you is better than a dog barking at you)

(Who does not have a dog is attacked by wolves).

(Better than Quais for his aunt)

Sabat Bin El Gouzy (deceased : 1256 AD) quoted by Quais: who is a man from Kufa, visited his aunt on a cold night, her house was narrow and she had a dog. Then, she let the dog enter the house and expelled Quais. Then, he died from coldness.

(Dog patience)

Nasr Bin Sayyar (deceased : 748 AD) said: the Greats of Turks said: "the morals of some animals should characterize the great leader: the cock generosity, the chicken compassion, the lionheart, the pig durability, the fox trickery, the dog patience on injury, the crane guarding, the raven caution, the wolf deceitfulness and the pigeon guidance."

It is said also that the pigeon is replaced by the sparrow chick, which is a small animal living in Khorasan getting weight when it is tired and exhausted.

(Dog rudeness)

Imam Ahmed Bin Ishaq El Sarmary (deceased : 856 AD) says: ten features should characterize the commander of invaders: he should have the lionheart not to be coward, the tiger pride not to humble, the bear courage killing by all its body parts, the pig durability not to escape, the wolf attack not to give up, the ant way of holding weapons as it holds weapons heaviest than it, the rock stability, the donkey patience, the dog rudeness; it goes to hell if its prey is there and the cock opportunity seeking.

Khosrow Anushirvan (deceased : 579 AD) said to Bozorgmehr (deceased : the sixth century): who taught you morals?

He said: my talent. I used all I found good in others and overcame what I found evil. I got the good features in everything:

I took from the dog its gregariousness for its owners and defended its wives.

Determination from being young from the pig

Help from the monkey

Patience from the donkey

Cautious from the raven

Kindness when required and soft voice from the cat

Al Tartooshy (deceased : 1126 AD) says:

Al Rabahy said: Hey, sons of Rabah, do not belittle any simple thing you take from its characteristics. I took from the fox its trickery, from the monkey its plots, from the jungle cat its panic, from the dog its power and the jackal its caution. I learned from the moon waking at night and from the sun appearing from time to time.

Abu Taher El Salafy (deceased : 1180 AD) says:

Sheikh Abu Bakr El Bashnawy: I learned the bully from the cock, the loyalty from the dog and the durability from the donkey.

Don't you see that when feed is brought to the cock, it crows to the female and it does not eat in secrecy, the dog feels grateful to you if you feed it one time, and the donkey tolerates your abuse without shouting or crying if you hit it, do not feed it or ride it.

4

Dogs are Preferred to Many of Those who wore Clothes

The book entitled "Dogs are Preferred to Many of Those Wearing Clothes" is the main book narrating the stories of dogs in the Arab Heritage written by the author, historian, translator, and literature specialist; Mohamed Bin El Marzaban (deceased : 921 AD).

The historian, Yaquot El Hamawy El Romy (deceased : 1229 AD) said: a translator was translating the Persian books into Arabic. He has more than fifty quotations from the Persian books.

The historian; Ibn Kathir El Korashy (deceased: 1373 AD) said about him: he has his special choice and etiquette. He classified a lot of books in advisable arts. He is the classifier of the book entitled "Dogs are Preferred to Many of Those Wearing Clothes."

His elders and others were coming to him, staying in his house and eating food with him, etc. The state superior was greeting him if he passed his house and stood until he came out to him.

Abu Ali El Faresy says about him: he is one of the advantages of life.

There are many narrations on the author's order of his book; some narrations were at his time, some were written decades ago, and some were written centuries ago.

It seems that our author suffered a lot from people's staleness and denial to his friendliness to them, which appear in the introduction of his book.

Ibn El Marzaban says:

The author shows the reason for writing the book:

You, May Allah Cherish You, show our time and the lack of affection, immorality, and vileness of its people. Good people were so far.

And who wants a friend without any lapse and pleasured all the time is a person taking a confusing way that the more effort he does, the farther he becomes from his target. This is true, as you described.

It was quoted on Abi Dhar El Ghaffary (May Allah pleased with him) that he said: "People were leaves without thorns. Then, they become thorns without leaves".

Some of them said: We were afraid that the plenty of giving appointments and need for apologizing make brothers forced to lie in giving appointments and mix their apologizing with exaggeration. Today, no one apologizes well and who was apologizing for guilt,

Lobaid said:

Those who are living with us left .. and I stayed alone as the scabby skin

One day, Bashar Bin Al Hareth was depressed and remained silent until the sunset. Then, he raised his head and said:

Ideal men denying all evil left

And I am living with those who deceive each other to defeat each other, and they are all disreputable

Here is a song of another person:

Those who are pleased when they find me coming and say welcome me

And still, those who are frown when find me coming and say if only he did not come

He also says:

You, May Allah, the Almighty cherish you, asked me to collect for you all narrations about the preference of the dog to the evil brothers and its good hidden and shown characteristics, as you collected all its features adequately and in detail.

Also, he says:

Be aware, May Allah cherish you that the dog is for his owner more compassionate than the parent on his child and the full brother on his brother as it guards its master and protects his wives when he is present, absent, slept, and awake. It does not stop it even if they harden it. It does not let them down even if they let it down.

It was narrated to us that a man asked a wise man for advice, and the wise man said: renounce pleasure in worldly things and do not dispute with people on them and be sincere for the sake of Allah like the dog which is sincere with its owners as it refuses not to be sincere while they let it hungry and hit it.

Omar Bin Shoaib quoted his father and grandfather saying: Allah's Messenger, Peace, and Blessings of Allah Be Upon Him, saw a killed man. Then, he said: ((Why was this man killed?)). They said: Oh Allah's Messenger, Peace, and Blessings of Allah Be Upon You: he leaped on the sheep of Abi Zahra and took a sheep, and then the sheepdog leaped on him and killed him. Allah's Messenger, Peace, and Blessings of Allah Be Upon Him said: he was killed by himself, lost his religion, disobeyed his lord, the Almighty, betrayed his brother and the dog was better than this betrayer)). After that, Allah's Messenger, Peace, and Blessings of Allah Be Upon Him said: ((Does any of you fail to protect his brother in Islam and his brother's family like this dog which protected the sheep of its masters))

The best friend

Omar Bin Al Khattab, May Allah be pleased with him, saw a Bedouin riding a dog. Then, he said: what is with you?

He said: Oh, Commander of Believers: it is the better friend. If you give it, it thanks you, and if you deprive it, it becomes patient.

Omar said: it is the best friend. Never let it go.

It is the one thanking me and keeping my secret

Abdullah Bin Omar Bin El Khattab, May Allah be pleased with them, saw a dog with a Bedouin. Then, he said to him: what is with you?

He said: it is the one thanking me and keeping my secret

He said: Keep your friend

El Ahnaf Bin Qays said: if the dog moves its tail, trust that it shows friendliness to you; while never trust the people's care as they may be deceivers.

The dog does not dissemble in its love.

El Shaby said: the best character in the dog is that it does not dissemble in its love.

Honest dog

Bin Abbas, May Allah be pleased with them, said: an honest dog is better than a traitor man.

Better than an evil companion

Gafar Bin Soliman said: I saw a dog with Malek Bin Dinar, and then I wondered: What is this!

He said: it is better than an evil companion.

It protects me from itself

Ishak Bin Ibrahim El Mosely said: one day, I came to El Fadl Bin Yahya; however, he was at the water source with a dog,

Then, I said to him: Are you walking with a dog!

He said: yes, it protects me from itself and others; it thanks me for little things and protects my house when I sleep and when I take a nap

Dogs die when their owners die due to sadness

Some narrators said: El Rabie Bin Badr raised a dog, and when El Rabie died, the dog was hitting his grave until it dies.

Amer Bin Antara has hunting dogs and sheep and he was treating them well. When he died, the dogs still at his grave until they died there while his family and relatives left.

Dog loyalty to who helped it

There was a dog following El Aamash until he gets back to home. When he was asked about this dog, he said: I saw boys hitting it, and I separated between them and then it recognized that and thanked me as it was moving its tail and following me wherever he saw me.

If El Aamash had been alive until our time and saw people now, his love for his dog would have increased.

If you saw a dog, keep it.

It was narrated that it is said that: people in our time are pigs. If you met a dog, keep it as it is better than the people at this time.

A man dying is enjoining his sons to care for his dog

El Asmaey said: some Bedouins attended the dying situation, and a dog was sitting at a corner in the house.

Then, he said to the eldest of his sons: I urge you to treat it well because it has favors I still thankful for; it guides my guest to me at darkness if the fire is put out.

He praises his dogs by poetry as they do not harm his guests.

Ibrahim Bin Herma has dogs smiling at his guests and not barking. They also move their tails between the guests' hands. Then, he praises them as follows:

In the darkness, my guest is guided by fire or dog barking

Moving their tails when they see and recognize him

And welcoming who they recognized as they are about to say hello to them

A king says: I would sacrifice my life for you!!

El Asmaey said: I heard some kings running behind a dog and became near to an Antelope saying happily: I would sacrifice my life for you.

Abu Nawas said:

They sacrifice and protect you ….they are the titles and their features

It has benefits more than harm

The dog's benefits are more than its harm; May Allah support you. Its benefits exceed and exaggerate its harm. Judges, jurists, worshippers, and hermits who enjoin what is right and forbid what is wrong, do not deny keeping dogs.

Who knows nothing says that the dog is a beast!

It is quoted from Omar Bin El Khattab; May Allah be pleased with him that those who know nothing says the dog is a beast. If it were a beast, it would not be familiar with people, afraid of beasts, hate death, familiar with the houses, and fear from prairie and wastelands.

How it is not like that while it is not satisfied by sleeping and lying on the ground. Wherever it finds any carpet or pillow, it lies on it. It always sits in a clean place as it selects the best positions in the council protected by its owner.

The dog knows its owner

I said: the dog and wild cat know their owners, their names and houses, and they are familiar with their places. If they are expelled, they come back. If they are let hungry, they are patient. If they are insulted, they tolerate it.

The dog's good characteristics also include that it looks at his owner's face, stares at his eyes and face. It loves him and be always near to him even it may tickle him and his boys by biting without any hurt or effect. It has teeth that can make tracks in the trees.

The neighborhood dogs bark and their sounds are followed

Abu Bakr El Sedik said: if a man in the desert loses his way and it becomes dark, he barks as dogs, then the district dogs bark, and he follows their sounds until he reaches the district.

A dog sacrifices and rescues its owner from inevitable death

A man came to some sultans, and he was accompanied by the governor of Armenia backing to his home. Then, he passed by a grave with a built-up dome where there was a statement; "this is a dog grave and who want to know its story can go to so-and-so village where he can be told.

The man asked about this village, and he was guided to it and asked its people and then they guided him to the Sheikh, and he sent to him and brought him. He found him an older man exceeding one hundred years. Then, he asked him.

And he said: yes, in this area, there was a great king who was known for hiking, hunting and traveling. He had a dog raised and named by him. He did not leave him. At his lunch and dinner times, he fed it from his food. One day, he went hiking and said to some of his servants: tell the chef to make porridge with milk as I desired it.

Then, he went hiking.

The chef brought milk, made to him a great porridge, forgot to cover it and worked on cooking something else

A snake came out of the cracks of fields and spilled out its poison in the porridge while the dog was lying, seeing all that as it couldn't prevent the snake.

The king has a dumb old slave-woman who saw what was made by the snake.

The king returned from hunting, and then he said: Hey servants, bring to me at first the porridge. When it is brought to him, the dumb slave-woman nodded but they did not understand what she was saying; the dog barked, but the king was not careful but it continued shouting to explain to them what it wanted. Then, the king threw to its food as usual, but the dog did not approach it and continued shouting.

He said to his servants: keep it away as it has a story and started eating the milk. When the dog saw him want to eat, it jumped to the table and entered its mouth in the milk and sipped from it. Then, it died, and its body became scattered.

The king was astonished by it and its behavior. Then, the dumb slave-woman nodded, and they understood the significance of the dog act.

The king said to his companions and bodyguards that this animal that sacrificed itself for me is worth a reward, and no one would carry and bury it but me. He buried it before its father and mother and built a dome on which the statement you read was written. This is its story.

Dog is grateful

A sincere older man narrated that he made pilgrim one year saying: we rested in Al Yaserreya and sat to have lunch, and a dog was lying near to us and then we threw to it some food we ate then we went and stayed in the king river. Days later, we found the dog lying near to us like the first day.

I said to the servants: this dog followed us, and it deserves to be kept by us and they promised him.

The servants spent the trip with it as it ate and followed us from house to house, and if anyone approached our camels and baggage, it barked and shouted.

We escaped from "Selal" to Mecca and determined to go to Yemen for work, and it was with us until we reached Quba and returned to Al Salam City, and it was with us.

A dog breastfed a kid!!

Ibn Abi Al Dunya narrated that the sweeping plague attacked a house people, the country people were sure that there was no one; young or old there.

A small baby boy was crawling and could not stand, and all the remaining people there turned towards the house door and blocked it without realizing the baby.

After months, the group successors transferred to the house, and when the door opened and they entered the house, a baby was playing with the puppy of a female dog owned by the house owners.

When the baby saw it, it crawled to it, and it breastfed it.

They recognized that the baby stayed in the house, became forgotten, was very hungry, and saw the dog breastfeeding its puppy, then it came to it, and when it breastfed it once, he was accustomed to it and asked her for feed always.

The narrator said: I saw this baby in Al Basra Mosque, and he was ravenous.

It was said that: this plague spread in the year of Sixty Nine.

A dog deprives itself of its food and sacrifices itself for its owner

Bin Shaddad narrated that: El Qasem has made me the successor of Ahmed Bin Maimoun at Neyshabur. Then, I stayed in a house there, and I found near to me a soldier friend of him called Nassim

He had a dog leaving when he leaves and entering when he enters. When it sat at his door, he approached it and covered it with a thick coat of him.

Then, I asked about the boy's place and how he could persuade the Prince to let the dog enter into his house and be satisfied by this while it is not a hunting dog.

Abu El Waleed said: ask him, and he would tell you. Then, I brought the boy and he asked him for the reason that makes the dog deserve this position.

Then, he said: this dog saved me from a serious matter; however, I found this saying unfamiliar and denied it.

He said to me: listen to his talk, and you will excuse me.

I was accompanied by a man from the people of Basra called Mohamed Bin Bakr, not leaving me, providing me with the wine for years. Al Deenor group expelled us, and when we backed and were near to our house, I had a purse around my waist containing some dinars and had a lot of belongings from the booty.

We reached a place where we ate and drank. When he made a drink to me intentionally, he pulled my hands and legs, bound me, threw me in a valley, took all I had, and left me alone.

I was depressed, and this dog sat with me, then it left me. After a short time, it brought me a loaf and put it between my hands; and I ate it.

I was crawling to a place where there was water, and I drank from it. The dog stayed with me all night, barking to the morning. I felt sleepy.

I lost the dog. After a short time, it brought me a loaf. Then, I ate and made what I made on the first day.

On the third day, it was absent, and I thought that it would bring a loaf to me. After a short time, it brought me a loaf and threw it to me, and I found my son before finishing eating it.

Then, he said: what are you doing here, and what is your story?

Then, he leaned and untied my shoulders, and I said to him: how did you know my place and who guided you?

He said: the dog has been coming to us daily, and we offered to it a loaf but it did not eat the loaf. It was with you and we denied that it returned without you. It was holding the loaf by its mouth and did not taste it, left and ran. We denied its matter. Then, I followed it until I reached you. This was the story of the dog and me. It is better for me than the family and relatives.

He said: I found ugly effects on his shoulders.

The messenger dog

Abu El Hussein Bin Shaddad said: I directed to Mukharek's monastery to Abdullah Bin El Tabary El Nasrany who was bringing guests to El Mutad Bellah. Then, I asked him to bring an agent called Ibrahim Bin Daran and demanded him to bring the guides to save a village known as Basiry El Sufla.

Then, he said to me: Sir, I sent one.

I said to him: I am sitting on the road, and no one met me.

Then, he said to me: Did not you find the dog with us. I sent it. He insulted me, and I asked for forgiveness from Allah.

Then, he said: if the group does not come on time, you can kill me without being guilty. After an hour, the group came with the dog. Then, I asked how to instruct it to give a message.

Then, he said: I bind a patch in its neck, indicating what I need and direct it to the destination. Then, it intends to the group who will know the news and read the patch. Then, they comply with it.

The older woman, her smart dog, and the thief

A regretful thief said to me: I entered a city mentioned to me, and I seek anything to steal, but I did not found. I saw a wealthy banker and I did tricks until I stole his purse.

I escaped but nearby, there was an older woman with a dog who hugged, kissed and followed me.

And said: oh my dear, I ransomed you and the dog moved its tail and approached me. People stood looking at us.

The woman was saying: Oh my god. Look at the dog; it knows him. People were astonished and I doubt myself and thought that she breastfed me while I did not know her.

And she said: walk with me to the house, stay with me, and never leave me. I walked with her to her home, where young men were drinking and eating all fruits and plants. They welcomed me and let me sit with them.

They have valuable belongings. I intended to steal them and still gave them alcohol, and they were drinking until they and all the people in the house slept.

I stole their belongings, and when I was going to leave the house, the dog jumped on me like a lion and shouted and still barking until all sleeping people woke up. Then, I was embarrassed.

The next day, what was happened the day before repeated, and I was still thinking for a trick for the dog but in vain. When they slept, I stole as much as I could. Then, the dog blocked my way. I was trying for three nights to steal, and when I gave up, I took their permission to leave and said: May I leave because I am busy, May Allah reinforce you.

Then, they said: it is up to the old woman. Then, I tried to take her permit

However, she said: give me what you took from the banker and leave wherever you want. Don't stay in this city because no one can deceive me.

Then, she took the purse and let me go. I also found also a distant place to be saved from her. Therefore, I am confined to ask her for pocket money, and she paid to me pocket money and accompanied me until I am out of the city.

The dog was with her until I exceed the city boarders. She stopped and I continued and the dog followed me until I became far. Then, it returned and looked at me and I looked at it until it was unseen to me.

How it protected its owner from the one intending to choke him

Some sheiks from the people of the mountain told me: I was going with a group to Isfahan. When we were on our way, we passed with a destructive unoccupied hotel.

Suddenly, we heard a dog barking and there was disorder. Then, we entered together with the hotel, and there was a friend of ours from Fiji accompanying a dog all the time.

A person with anesthetic substance jumped to him but the Fijian was intelligent and when the person with anesthetic substance noted that, he put a string around his neck to squeeze his neck. When the dog saw that, it ran to the person with anesthetic substance, scratched his face, bit his nap and took flesh from him. Thus, the person with an anesthetic substance fainted.

We saved our friend by removing the string from his neck and it was about to be damaged, arrested the person with anesthetic substance, trussed him up by his string and pushed him to the sultan.

A dog helping its owner

Ibrahim Bin Barqan narrated to me that: there was a man from Isfahan called El Khaseeb near to us.

He had a dog bringing it from the mountain. He disputed with his neighbor until they quarreled.

When the dog saw that, it jumped to the man quarreling with its owner, put his claws in his eyes and bit his nap until I saw the man fainted and his blood was spread on the floor.

A dog preserves its owner's honor

Al Hareth Bin Sasaa is an example for a man whose companion made a relationship with his wife while his dog protected his honor. Al Hareth had two companions accompanying him all the time. He loved them. He sent one of them to his wife and Al Hareth had a dog raised by him.

Al Hareth was hiking with his companions and assigned that man to act on his behalf. When Al Hareth stayed away, his companion came to his wife and stayed at her house eating and drinking. When they got drunk and lied down and the dog saw that he was lied down on her belly, the dog jumped on them and killed them.

When Al Hareth returned to his house and saw them, he recognized what happened and said while he was at their grave:

It still cares for me, protects my wife...while my companion betrays me

I wonder that the companion dishonored consensual sex...I wonder that the dog preserved my honor

He left his companions and considered his dog a companion. Thus, the Arabs took him an exemplary. He said:

The dog is better than any friend betraying me and having sexual intercourse with my wife after I die

My dog will be my companion and I will provide it with all friendliness and kindness I have provided to my friend

A dog killed its master's wife and her mate

Al Hassan Bin Malek El Ghanawy had two companions like his brothers. one of them dishonored him. He had a dog sitting at his house door raised by him. One day, the man came to Al Hassan's house and entered to his wife's place.

She said to him: he was far away. Would you mind to stay with me?

He said: yes. Then, they ate and drank and when he started tohave sexual intercourse with her, the dog jumped on them and killed them. When Al Hassan backed and saw them in this case, he recognized what happened and said:

My companion betrayed me while I am friendly and kind with him

He started to have sexual intercourse with my wife after I considered him as my brother while my dog did not leave him until he was killed by it

A dog killed its master's wife and her lover

Al Asmaey said: Malek Bin El Waleed had companions. Then, he sent one of them to his wife and she accepted to have a relationship with him. One night, he hid in one of Malek's house where his wife was and Malek did not know anything.

When he started to have sexual intercourse with her, Malek's dog jumped on them and killed them; however, Malek was unconscious because he was drunk. When he woke up, he said while he was at their grave:

Each dog raised by you caring for you and protecting you as long as it is alive

Is better than a companion betraying you, stealing your money and having sexual intercourse with your wife after kindness

The dog preserves your honor for life

Sasaa Bin Khaled had a companion. One day, he found him killed in his bed with his wife. Thus, he recognized their betrayal and said:

The betrayal is the characteristic of each cad..and the dog preserves your honor

Let mean people go and keep your dog ...so that you will avoid betrayal and cunning

Two dogs protect their owner from the snake

Some friends of mine narrated to me: one night, I went out while I was drunk. Then, I went to the garden for a purpose with two dogs raised by me a stick.

When I was about to sleep, the two dogs started barking. Then, I woke up and did not see anything bad. Thus, I hit and expelled them and slept.

They barked again and awakened me, but I did not see anything bad. Thus, I jumped on and expelled them and slept.

They moved me by their hands and legs as awoke people move a slept man for a serious matter.

I leaped and suddenly saw a snake near to me. I killed it and went back to my house. Thus, the two dogs were my saver after Allah, the Almighty.

I was very sad for Mesmar

It is narrated that Maymouna, May Allah be pleased with her; the wife of Prophet Mohamed, Peace and Blessings of Allah Be Upon Him, had a dog called Mesmar.

She took it wherever she went so that no one can steal her baggage.

When she returned, she let it stay with Bani Gadila and spent on him. When he died and she was told, she cried and said: I was very sad for Mesmar.

He killed his faithful dog

A friend told me that he had a friend whose wife died and had a boy.

He had a dog raised by him. One day, he left his son in the house with the dog and went out for a purpose.

After one hour, he saw the dog in the lobby and its face and mouth were full of blood.

He thought that it killed his son and ate him. He killed the dog intentionally before it entered the house.

However, he found the boy slept and next to it the rest of a snake killed and eaten by the dog.

The man strongly regretted killing the dog and buried it.

5

Dog Stories in the Arab Heritage

In this chapter, we state some stories about dogs other than those mentioned by Ibn Marzipan. Some of the stories may not be heard by him and were mentioned by others. Some occurred after him. The stories are as follows:

The beginning of the relationship between dogs and humans

Wahb Ibn Munbih (died: 732 AD) said: When Adam (peace be upon him) came down to the earth where there were predators and insects, the devil came and said to them, "an animal came down to kill you so you should kill him. They surrounded Adam from all directions and he was terrified.

He said: O my God, protect me from them. Allah inspired him the following: Choose one of them to protect you, so he called the dog and patted his head. The dog opposed them and drove them away. Therefore, dogs make friends with the children of Adam and keep their vow.

The first to use the dog as a guard

It was narrated that 'Abd-Allaah (may Allaah be pleased with him) (deceased: 653 AD) said: The first to make the dog as a guard was Noah, peace be upon him. He said, "O God, you ordered me to build a ship and I spent days building it, but they came at night and ruin it. When shall I accomplish what you ordered me to do as time has been long? God inspired him the following:

"O Noah, use a dog as your guard, so Noah used a dog, and he worked at daytime and slept at night. If his people came to damage his work at night his dog barked at them and Noah peace be upon him took the cudgel and attacked them so they ran away from him. He, thus, achieved what he wanted.

Between a dog, a horse, and a falcon

It was narrated that Suleiman (peace be upon him) brought the drink of Paradise, and he was told: If you drink this you will not die.

He consulted with his servants, except the hedgehog; they all said: Drink.

Then he sent the horse and the falcon to the hedgehog calling it, but it did not answer them. Then, he sent it the dog, which it answered.

Sulaiman, peace be upon him said: Why did not you answer the horse and falcon?

It said: They are harsh! Because the horse runs with the enemy as with its owner, and the falcon obeys its non-owner as it obeys its owner, but the dog is loyal. Even if its owner expels it outside the house, it comes back again.

He said to it: should I drink this?

He said: Do not drink because it will make you live longer in prison, because dying in good status is better than living in prison.

The first king of Babylon ordered to use dogs to save livestock

The greatest historian of the Arabs, Al–Tabari (d. 923), says in his book, which is the basis of the Arab history books (*History of Nations and Kings*):

Scholars said that the first king of Babylon Tahmworth ... ordered to use dogs to save livestock and to guard them against the predators.

How were public figures dealing with dogs: -

A boy gives all his food to a dog

Abdullah bin Jaafar (deceased: 700 AD) went out to his estate and rested around the palms of some people where a black boy was working.

When the boy brought his food, a dog entered and approached him. the boy threw a pie to the dog and ate it. Then, he threw a second and a third, which the dog also ate, while Abdullah was looking.

He said, "Boy, what is your today's food?"

He said: what you have seen.

He said: Why did you give it to this dog?

He said: dogs do not live in this land. It must have come from a long distance feeling hungry, and I hated to be full while it was hungry.

He said, "What are you doing today?"

He said: my day ended.

Abdullah Ibn Ja'far wept and said: I should be blamed for lack of generosity. This boy is more generous than me so he bought the place, the boy, and the tools in it. Then, he set the boy free and gave him some tools.

The boy said: If that is for me, it is for the sake of Allah Almighty.

Abdullah thought well of the boy and he said: if he will be that generous, I should never be less generous.

The same story is told about his cousin, Al-Hasan Ibn 'Ali (d. 670 AD) and about Imam Muhammad bin Wasea (died: 741 AD).

A Sheikh approached the dog and did not approach the Imam

In the virtues of Imam Ahmad (d. 855 AD), he was informed that a man from behind the river had triple hadiths. Imam Ahmad traveled to him and found an old man feeding a dog. He greeted him and the Sheikh replied to his greetings. Then, the Sheikh was busy feeding the dog. The Imam felt hurt as the Sheik was more interested in the dog than him. When the Sheikh finished feeding the dog, he turned to Imam Ahmad and said: are you hurt because I was more interested in the dog more you?

He said: Yes.

The Sheikh said: Abu Al-Zanad quoted from Al-Arag who quoted from Abu Hurayrah (may Allah be pleased with him) who said that the Prophet (peace and blessings of Allaah be upon him) said: "Whoever shunned anyone who sought help, will be shunned by Allah on the Day of Resurrection and will never go to paradise."

Our land is not inhabited by dogs, and this dog has sought help from me. I was afraid to shun it so Allah would shun me on the Day of Resurrection.

Imam Ahmad said: This hadith is enough for me and he came back.

a dog puts its mouth on his knee

Scholars said: I came to Malik bin Dinar (deceased: 748 m) when he was sitting alone and I found a dog putting its mouth on his knee. I went to drive it away.

He said: Let it; this does not harm or hurt; it is even better than a bad companion.

He said:

People's harm if you think about it ... is more dangerous than a dog's harm

Because the dog does not hurt a companion ... and you are in torment all the time because of people's harm

The road between me and the dog is common

Some of the companions of Imam Ibrahim al-Firozabadi (d. 1083 AD) were walking with him on the way when a dog interrupted them.

The jurist said, "this dog is stupid." and he ousted it.

The Sheikh forbade him and said: "why did you drive it out of the way? Did not you know that the way between me and it is common?

He saw the dogs eating dates

Sheikh Ahmad al-Rifa'i (d. 1182 AD) passed by a food court and saw dogs eating dates from the pot and jostling so he stood at the door so that no one would harm them.

He saw a bitch that gave birth and died

Imam Majd al-Din Ibn Daqeeq al-Eid (d. 1302 AD) passed by and saw a bitch that gave birth and died.

He said to his student Taqei El-Dein Abdul-Malik al-Armanti (d. 1322 AD): "O Taqei, bring this carpet." He carried the puppies, put them in a nearby place and brought milk to feed them until they grew up. Similar incidents were told about him.

when people saw him, they said this is Abu Sadiq and his dog

Abu Sadiq Murshid Al-Maliki (died: 1123 AD), the hadith scholar.

He was very kind to animals, especially cats and dogs. He was the supervisor of the mosque where he made a servant take care of cats every day. In addition, at his home at Al-Akfal alley in Egypt, there were dogs that he fed and sometimes they follow his mount and walk with him in the markets.

Al-Shareef Muhammad bin Asaad Al-Jawani (d. 1192) said in the book, Al-Nokat on Al-khetat: Sheikh Munjib Ghulam Abu Sadiq told me: My master Sheikh Abu Sadiq had a dog that would never leave him. If he was riding, the dog would walk behind him. If his mule stopped, it stayed near its legs. Therefore, when people saw him, they said, "this is Abu Sadiq and his dog."

He told me, "A bitch gave birth in a bathroom stove, and the muezzin came after my master every day at the time before daybreak to read the Koran. My master took in his sleeve every day a loaf, came near to the bitch, took off his cloak, cut bread and threw it for the bitch to eat. Then, he called the stoker and gave him a carat saying to him: Wash her mug and fill it with sweet water, He made him swear to do it.

When its puppies grew up a little, he took two loaves until they grew up and dispersed.

He told me: He rented a shop to cats from the charity in the old mosque. He brought pieces of glands, sat down and distributed it to the cats. One of the cats carried some of it and went away, and it did it repeatedly. My master said to Sheikh Abi Al-Hassan bin Faraj, "go behind this cat and see where it goes with it. Ibn Faraj went after the cat and saw it giving the pieces to its kittens. He returned to him and told him. Afterward, he cut glands into as small pieces as the kitten can eat, in addition to the large pieces for big cats. He kept sending the small pieces to the kittens until they grew up.

It was said to a dog: O dog, son of a dog. His father replied: Why are you cursing him?

Shaykh Taj al-Din Ibn al-Sobki (d. 1370 AD) said in, *Al Tarsheh*: I was once in the corridor of our house with a company when a dog passed by and was dripping water that almost touched our clothes. I scolded it saying, "O dog son of a dog."

so Sheikh Imam means his father, Sheikh Taqi al-Din al-Subki (deceased: 1355 AD) heard us from inside and came out saying: Why are you cursing him?

I said: "I said only really; is not it a dog and son of a dog?

He said: yes, it is, but you say it like cursing and insulting; this is inappropriate.

I said: This is a benefit. No creature should be called by its quality unless it is not categorized as an insult.

He ordered the dog a hundred camel as blood money!

Asmaa Bin Kharga (deceased: 686 m) stayed at the back of Al-Kufa in a grassy meadow that he liked where there was a man from the sons of Abs. When he saw Asmaa' domes, the man demolished his house; Asmaa said to him: What is wrong with you?

He said: I have a dog that I love more than my son, and I am afraid that it harms you and some of your servants kill it.

He said to him: Stay and I am a protector of your dog; Asmaa said to his servants: If you see his dog reaching my bowl, none of you harm it.

They followed his orders. Then, Asmaa traveled and a man from sons of Asad stayed in the same meadow. When the dog came, as usual, the Asadi threw an arrow at it and was killed; Abssi came to Asmaa saying: What did the dog do?

He said: You killed it;

He said: And how?

He said: you made it have a habit that made the man kill it; you should order a hundred camels as blood money of the dog.

He described it in a way that made me wish I was a dog

Al-Asma'i (d. 831 AD) said I entered into al-'Atabi (d. 835 AD) as the commander of the faithful, Al-Ma'mun, had sent him to Al-Makhram. I found him sitting leaning and a dog was sitting between his arms. He was holding a mug of drink from which he took a sip and the dog licked.

I said to him: God bless you! Your old age, your knowledge and your status of being close to the commander of the faithful make you greater than having a drink with a dog!

He said: mind your own business! This is better than bad peers. It is patient with me whether I have a lot or few; it keeps me whether I am here or absent, and it protects me from its harm and others harm.

He said: he described it so beautifully that I wished I was a dog.

They said to him: Try it on a dog!

It was found in some books on morality by Al-Saheb Bin Ibad (deceased: 995 AD) that he once requested a drink, so he was given a mug. When he was about to drink, some of his friends said to him, "Do not drink; it is poisoned!"

He said to him: What is the evidence?

He said: Try it on who gave it to you!

He said: I do not think it is proper or halal.

He said: Try it on a dog!

He said: "mutilating animals is forbidden." He ordered to get rid of what was in the mug.

He said to the boy: "Go away and do not enter my house again", and he gave the boy his wage.

He said: Do not negate certainty by doubt and do not punish by cutting off livelihood is villainy.

Dogs reveal criminals: -

A dog reveals the murderer of its master

Judge Tannukhi (d. 994) said:

Abu Othman al-Madani said: In his neighborhood in Baghdad, there was a tribalist man playing with dogs.

He went out one day before dawn to get something and was followed by a dog that was favored to him. He tried to get it away, but the dog did refuse to leave him so he let it follow him.

On his way, he was stopped by some people who had enmity with him. They noticed that he was not armed, so they caught him, and the dog was watching. They took him inside and killed him. They buried him in a well in the house, and they beat the dog which ran outside. It came to the house of his owner howling, but they did not care about it.

The man's mother missed her son for a day and night, and she noticed the wounds of the dog. She realized that the one who did this to the dog killed her son and that he was lost. She arranged the funeral and drove the dogs away from her house

This dog remained at the door and did not leave so they sometimes checked on it.

One day, one of the killers of the owner passed by the door where the dog was lying. The dog recognized him and attacked, bit and grabbed his leg.

The passers-by tried hard to release him but they could not. The noise rose, and the guard of the road came; he said, why is this dog grabbing the man? There must be a story behind it, and perhaps he is the one who injured it.

The mother of the slain came out. When she saw the man, and the dog attaching to him and heard the guard's words, she looked carefully at the man. She remembered that he was one of the enemies of her son.

She thought that he killed her son, so she gripped him, and claimed that he was the murder. They went to the police officer who locked the man. Although he was hit, he did not admit the murder. However, the dog stayed at the door of a prison.

After days, the man was released, and when he came out of the custody door, the dog hung him, as it did first. The people wondered about it.

The police officer secretly ordered some of his men to part the dog and the man and to follow the man, know his destination, and observe him. They did so.

The dog kept following the killer that was also followed by the policemen until he is at home.

The police get into the house but they did not find a trace.

The dog came yelling and looking at the location of the well where the dead man was thrown.

The policeman said: dig up the place where the dog is digging. They did so and found the man dead.

The man was arrested and beaten so he confessed and told about the group of killers. He was killed and the rest were summoned, but they fled.

A Dog reveals its owner's killers

Ibn Tulun (d. 884 AD), the governor of Egypt, had a high-looking palace to which he ascended on hot nights.

Once late at night, he heard the bark of a dog at his door. The bark got louder so he ordered his servants to drive it away, but it came back again. Then, they went out and beat it. However, it resumed barking more loudly.

Then Ibn Tulun sat down and said, "This dog has news!"

He commanded a servant of his own that's known for his reasonability and understanding. He said to him, "This dog has news; go out and take a group of boys from the house and follow this dog; go with it and inform me about its news!

He said; the servant went out with a group of boys from the house. When the dog saw them, it waged its tail, and they followed it to an Egyptian neighborhood in Dabq alley

The dog stood at a closed house's door, started to dig again with his hands, barked, and pushed the door with his head.

The servant ordered to break that door to get into the house, and they found a dead girl and six men.

They immediately brought them to stand before Ibn Tulun. They admitted that they meet to have a drink and bring prostitutes to get their end away. Then, they kill her and take her jewelry and clothes, and they did so to that girl.

He asked about the dog; her parents told him that she raised it when it was still a puppy, and it never left her; it was with her wherever she went at any time.

He ordered to bring the men, and they were nailed after cutting their hands. They were tied by their throats, put on camels that went around carrying them until they perished.

A dog reveals the sheep's owner

Ibn Hamdun (d. 1167 AD) said that some Arabs were given the authority of policing neighborhoods of the Arabs and taking care of their affairs.

Two people sought to have him judge between them about sheep, each claiming to be the owner, and no one testified for one of them.

He ordered them to put the sheep in a place – where there was a dog belonging to the owner of the sheep - and to stay nearby.

He came to them at night; he said to one of them, "Go, and bring me one of the sheep."

So he went, but the dog barked at him so he returned back again.

He said to him: stay at your place.

And he called the other and said, "Go, bring me one of them."

He brought it and the dog did not bark at him. Therefore, it was judged that the sheep belonged to him.

A dog reveals the real husband

They mentioned that an old man went out with his young wife. They headed to Hammad castle. He was accompanied on the way by a young man who was in love with that wife and she also loved him. They conspired to claim that they were married to get rid of the old man.

When they arrived at the castle, that old man complained to Hammad (died: 1029 AD) about his problem and described his condition with them.

Hammad faced the young man and the woman, and they confirmed that they were married and denied what the old man claimed.

So Hammad asked the old man, if anyone accompanied them on their way, or if he had proof.

He said: "No one other than this dog accompanied us on our way," pointing to a dog that was with him.

He ordered the old man to tie the dog to date or wedge that was there. Then, he ordered the woman to untie it, so she went and sent the dog.

Then, he ordered her to tie the dog, which did not resist any of that.

Then, he said to the young man: go, untie the dog and then tie it.

When he was about to do this, the dog barked and resisted. He said to the woman: "This is your husband, the old man and this evildoer comes to after your husband."

He ordered to decapitate the young man.

A dog that recognizes the traitorous wife

Al-Zahaby, the historian, (deceased: 1348 m) said a Bedouin person had a cousin that was extremely beautiful. He got poor and traveled with her. On his way, he met a Senhadji prince, who picked her up out of pity on them. Then, the prince went away fast. When the Bedouin arrived at the Prince's house, he was shunned, so he went to the king who said to that prince: "return his wife back".

He denied, and said: "O Bedouin! Do you have a witness, even a dog, that knows her?"

He said: Yes.

He entered with a dog he owned into the house, and the women were brought out. When the dog saw her, he knew her and wagged its tail, so the king ordered that she be given to the Bedouin and that the prince is decapitated.

The Bedouin said: "She is divorced because she was silent and satisfied."

The king said: "You are right, and if you had not divorced her, I would have done to you as I did to him."

Then he ordered to bring the woman, and she was killed.

The following two stories are similar to the story mentioned by Ibn al-Marzban (died: 921 AD), about the sacrifice of this strange and loyal animal: -

The first story:

Abu Usman Saeed bin Salam Al Moqree (deceased: 983 m) said: during my early days at Sicily, I had a horse and a dog to hunt beasts. One day, I was about to drink milk from my bottle, but my dog barked and jumped at me fiercely preventing me from drinking milk.

I was surprised by its deed and waited. Then, I tried again to drink.

The dog jumped at me again, when I tried to drink for the third time, the dog jumped at the bottle and drank the milk, but it died immediately!!

Perhaps the dog saw a snake put its head in the milk, so it sacrificed itself for my sake. It became the cause of my repentance and my involvement in this issue. The loyalty of that dog is worth meditation.

The Second Story:

Bin Abdel Hady (deceased: 1503 AD), the Author of Alienation on Dogs Situations, says:

I was told that once a group of harvestmen went to harvesting with a glass of milk. they put it somewhere and were engaged in harvesting, and a snake came out of a hole directing to the milk. It drank the milk and vomited it in the glass.

When they returned for lunch, a dog with them; witnessing that, was preventing them from eating and running towards the snake hole. However, they did not realize it and did not turn to it.

As they were not aware of what happened and wanted to eat the milk and exhausted the dog, it preceded them and drank it. it died and his flesh was separated from his bones.

they realized that it was directing them to that, and it protected them by itself.

A Dog calling dogs for a feast!

El Demiry (deceased: 1405 AD) narrated in his book; Animal Great Life, about some Sufism that: We were in Tarsus. we met and get out to Bab El Jihad. a dog from the country followed us. When we reached to Bab El Jihad, we saw a dead animal. we ascended to space and sat down.

When the dog saw the dead animal, he went back to the country. he returned with about twenty dogs.

When they reached the dead animal, this dog sat somewhere and the dogs were eating it greedily until they got satisfied while this dog still looking at the dead animal until there were only bones. When the dogs backed to the country, this dog ate the remaining flesh in the bones. it leaves.

Two Knights and a Dog

It was said to Hatem El Taey (deceased: 578 AD): have you seen anyone more generous than you?

He said: Yes, no one should be arrogant and proud when dealing with any creature on earth. There are differences between creatures.

It was said to him: How come?

He said: once upon a time, I got out for work. I reached to a meadow and brook. I saw a man sitting with his horse in his hand and his spear at his side, and there was food in front of him and he was eating.

When he saw me, he greeted me and invited me saying: please get down! Then I got down and saw a lot of food in front of him enough for a group. we ate.

When we were satisfied, he threw all the food in the sand and we both rode our horses. He asked me, after that, about my destination and I told him.

he said: and this is also my destination.

I said: Oh, group example, why did you throw the food while we were on a trip, and we needed it?

He smiled and said: Never think in the bread of the next day. Each day has new bread as long as you have a long life.

Hatem said: we walked. On the next day, he opened my food by his hand and we ate on the brookside.

He threw the food to this brook. Suddenly, a dog came from the desert wanting water.

When it reached and saw the food, it ate until it was satisfied, drank from the brook and left the remaining food.

My companion said to me: Look, guy, this animal ate until it was satisfied only – while it is an animal – left the remaining food without being exhausted?! Was the dog smarter than us?

I said: while I was astonished: You did well.

We reached to the land as the next day started; we were surrounded by space and felt starving.

I said to myself: From where would we have lunch?

And I praised him for his act. While I am talking to myself, the dog was running as I thought that its group is near, however, it killed a group of zebra and gave them to us as we imagined that it was saying: this group is for you.

We took from it until we were satisfied, slaughtered, grilled and ate with the dog.

On the next day, we came to Arab districts. We saw a large group of ships and camels. We stroke them by spears. They ran into us. We kept away. When we looked back, the group knights were running into us. The dust spread behind us. We backed to meet the group.

When my companion saw me intending to meet the group with him, he smiled at me and said:

Guy, for the sake of Al-Lat and Al-Uzza, stand in this place, keep the booty and let me as I was encouraged by your support. If I am defeated, recover me.

He said: I stood with the booty keeping it for an hour. The horses withdrew and he was at the back shouting as champions without any fear from a large number of men. Many of them were killed and injured. He returned to me as a victorious lion.

Hatem said: we took the brook to the place where we made our friendship. The dog did not leave us.

At this place, the ship and booty were divided by him to three thirds, and I witnessed him.

He said: Guy, choose your share, take it and call your relatives, then I said:

Oh, my master. It is not fair to take even one piece from this booty; however, you divided it into three thirds, who are the third person?

He said while smiling: this dog

I said: How can these ships and camels benefit this dog?

He said: it can benefit from them as it wants because it became our companion in giving us the group of zebra. It also ate from our food. I had to support it. Take your share and go to your family, and I would do the same. Who will be followed by the dog would take its share acting in it at his discretion.

When I heard this, I was astonished and felt that it is a good act.

When both of us left with his share, the dog followed me.

He said: hey, Guy, take the dog's share for you.

I added it to my share.

When we went away, he ran towards me. I said: I sear he regretted his act and returned to take its booty.

I left it and said: this is your booty, idols bless it.

He said: oh Guy. Never do that. Do not characterize me with meanness and unfairness. I only returned to you to ask for your name and surname as we became companions and relatives, and I still did not know your name and you also did not ask me out of your kindness. My name is Attaf Ibn Qabed El Tary, and you?

I said: I am Hatem Bin Saad El Taey. Once he heard my name, he got down and said: Excuse me, the Master of Tayy, I heard about you and your generosity for years. I hoped for meeting you and I did my best to follow you. He mixed his arrow with my arrow and said:

Hatem, do not return it; for the sake of Al-Lat and Al-Uzza, my sword would benefit you. I would be pleased if you come with me to my country to give you an additional one thousand ships.

He said: I thanked him and gave my family this booty.

Dog and Monkey

Erwa Al Zobairy performed pilgrimage in 924 AD. He bought a monkey from Mecca, and his brother-in-law had a dog. The monkey familiarized the dog as they were eating in one place.

He said: Al Quormoty waylaid us, we took the sword, people separated and became away from their luggage. I escaped and came to Kufa without any dirham.

Once upon a time, I was sitting thinking who I can ask and what I can work, I found the noise.

I went out to see the monkey riding the dog, they came together to Kufa and people were laughing.

The monkey was feeding the dog, wanting to ride it and cheated on it to do it all the way.

When I saw the monkey and the dog, I called them and they came to me.

People said: what is this?

I said: they are mine. I took them.

The Prince of Kufa was informed. he sent it to me for selling them.

I sold them against Three Hundred Dirhams which was the reason for my welfare at that time. I went out of the country.

Dogs and Lion

The Indian King sent to Haroun Al Rasheed (deceased: 809 AD) fortress swords, dogs with straps and Indian clothes.

When the messengers gave him the gift, he ordered the Turkish People to make two lines in order that only their pupils can be seen. He allowed the messenger to enter, then he said to them: what did you bring?

They said: this is the best of our clothing. Haroun has ordered the person cutting to cut a lot of covers and veils from them to his horse. He crucified the messengers on their faces. They were ashamed.

The concierge said to them: What else do you have?

They said to him: these are unique fortress swords. Haroun called for the hard sword; the sword of Amr Bin Moed Yakrab (deceased: 642 AD), then all swords were cut by it one by one as radish without any flexion in its blades. He threatened them to be killed by the sword. He crucified that group on their faces.

He said to them: What else do you have?

They said: these are dogs with straps that can slaughter lions.

Haroun said to them: I have a lion. If they slaughtered it, you are right.

He ordered to bring a lion. it went out. When they looked at it, they were terrified and said to him: we do not have such a lion in our country!

Haroun said to them: these are our lions.

They said: let's direct the dogs towards it.

The dogs were three. They were directed to it and ripped it.

Haroun admired them and said to them: take anything you want from our country.

They said: we do not want anything but the hard sword by which our swords were cut.

He said to them: this is not allowed in our doctrine to give you a weapon as a gift; otherwise, we would give it to you. However, wish anything else.

They said: we do not wish anything but it.

He said: No way! he ordered a lot of antiques for them and rewarded them well.

A Dog preying on a lion!

A dog was described to Al Motawakel (deceased: 861 AD) by Armenia preying on the lion. He sent it back by the messenger.

Al Toraihy said to him: Oh, Commander of Believers, Congratulations on what Allah has assigned to you including obtaining your needs, having your loved people and anything desired by the Commander of Believers is assigned to him and increased by his prayers to Allah.

Al Motawakel said to him: this is for you as a reward for this congratulation. You can buy it in your capacity.

He bought it by him against two thousand Dinars. he put it on a lion and they attacked each other until they died.

A dog serving a big blind dog

Bin Abdel Hady (deceased: 1503 AD), the Author of Alienation on Dogs Situations, says:

When we were young, we had a red dog in the street.

One person came and threw to it a loaf of bread, it took it and when a big blind dog passed, it gave it to it. Another dog came and took it from the big blind dog. The red one went to the one took it and got it from it. It came to give it to the blind one and sat looking at it and protecting it from dogs until it ate it,

An intelligent dog obeying orders

Bin Abdel Hady (deceased: 1503 AD), the Author of Alienation on Dogs Situations, says:

Our neighbors had a black dog called: Zaytoun. It was obeying all their orders.

They had an orchard. Sometimes, they were saying to it: go and sit in the orchard. It went in time to it.

On some nights, they were saying to it: go this night sleep in the orchard. it went to sleep there this night.

Sometimes, they were saying to it: don't come tomorrow, stay in the orchard. it stayed all day and did not come. It obeyed anything ordered by them without violating it.

A dog driving horses

In (869 AD), Yaquob Bin El Laith (deceased: 879 AD) entered Fares, possessed it and got Ali Bin Quraish as a prisoner.

Jacob, as mentioned by historians, is one of the world champions and one of the adult shrewd princes 1.

Jacob won in Ali's battle against Ali. Ali had to take caution as he knew that he is the target of Jacob. He believed that Yaquob was coming to Fares and he was on that day in Shiraz located at Fares.

He stayed at a narrow place under a mountain confined to only one man. There is a wide river on the other side. He left Shiraz conquered by him and said: if Yaquob came, he could not reach us because of access was difficult.

Jacob came until it became near to the river. he ordered his companions to get down for about one mile of the river following Kerman.

He came with a spear in his hand and only one man.

He looked at the river, mountain and road and observed the soldiers of Ali Bin El Hussein. Ali's companions were insulting him, and he was silent without any reply.

When he observed all he wanted and saw it, he backed to his companions.

Tomorrow at the noon, he came with his soldiers and men until he went to the river beach following Karman land, and ordered his companions who got down their animals and left their baggage.

He opened a box with him while people were looking at him. They took out a predator. They get their animals up naked and took their spears in their hands.

He said: it was said that this would be the fate of the companions of Ali Bin El Hussein, and they made lines on the passage between the mountain and river, and they believed that Yaquob cannot access to another way.

They threw the dog in the river while Ali's companions were looking at it and laughing at them.

When they threw the dog in it, it was swimming in the water beside the soldier of Ali Bin El Hussein. Yaquob's companions broke into their naked animals behind the dog having their spears in their hands tracking the dog.

When Ali Bin El Hussein saw that Yaquob has crossed the river to reach to him, he was confused.

Yaquob's companions came from behind the river. Ali Bin Al Hussein and his companions were defeated, injured and directed to Kerman.

Ali Bin Al Hussein's animal tumbled and he fell. some boys put his turban in his neck and withdrew him to Yaquob who chained and imprisoned him. Jacob entered into Shiraz.

Dogs bearing fire to its owners!

I conclude the book with a very painful story of one of the wicked leaders who is an example for the saying: the end justifies the means. He was a bloody unjust ruler and the upper arm of the country (deceased: 983 AD)

The historian, Meskoey (deceased: 1030 AD) says in his book; the Experiences of nations and succession of inspiration:

One of his plots is being called the upper arm of the country commonly repeated as he plotted a group of the cage and Baloch people when he overwhelmed in Kerman to evacuate them from it.

The result was that a group of them has houses behind a mountain as they are non-accessible unless passing a strait. If a few numbers of people stood, they prevent a lot of soldiers from standing.

We lost hope in reaching it by force, he made a trick and threatened them that they should pay a royalty.

They said: we do not have money for you.

He said: you are hunters and I want a dog from each house.

So they had to do it. He counted their houses and took dogs of the same number.

The dog is sheltered by its master and still moving its tail for and around him. It also rubs him and be familiar with his house as if it escaped from a lot of parsecs, it returned to its coach.

He was ordered to put in their necks white oil rings and gather them in the mountain strait. The fire struck in oil and released and followed by the military.

They did that and the dogs were running quickly and the group felt that the soldiers were coming. They met them in the strait and each dog was sheltered by its master from fire.

When it rubbed the man, the fire spread and the road became accessed. The dogs followed them, and the fire passed. A lot of them were fired.

The dogs attacked the houses, the occupiers of them evacuated, the soldiers followed them quickly, prepared sword and eradicated their apartheid.

Conclusion

In the end, I hope that I have succeeded to combine this collection of books from our great heritage about this animal famous for its loyalty.

I have gathered as much information as I could. However, I am certain that the stories of dogs in Arab heritage are many more than what I have collected.

There are many manuscripts that have not been verified and have not been organized into printed books. I hope these manuscripts are not missing; they include the following:

Ibn Qutayba al-Dinuri (died: 889 AD), the author of *Al-Tasaneef*, has a book entitled: (The Dogs).

The same author wrote a book titled *Literature of Writers*, one of the four books that Ibn Khaldun (d. 1406AD) said that they are the four pillars of the Literature.

About the other book, the writer Salah al-Din al-Safadi (died: 1363 AD) mentioned a book titled: (Preferring the ethics of dogs over the people of distinction and mistrust who are most in need to reprimand) by Muhammad Ibn Umar al-Muqari, the writer.

Also, there are many books that were unfortunately lost, either because of hatred, millions of them were burned by enemies, or because of the neglect of the descendants.

There are also many books that are still manuscripts, which have not been verified or published.

I hope that the nation regains the glories of the ancestors, renew their treasure, and preserve this great heritage.

Resources and references

1- Al-Mofadel Al-Dabi (died: 784 AD): *Amthal Al-Arab (Proverbs of the Arabs)* - Al-Hilal House and Library - Edition: First, 1424 AH.

2- Al-Shafi'i (died: 820 AD): *Al-Om (the Mother)* – Dar Almarefa - Publishing Year: 1410AH / 1990AD.

3- Abdul Malik Bin Hisham (died: 828 AD): *Al-Tigan in Molouk Hamir (Crowns in the Himyarite kings)* - publisher: Center for Yemeni Studies and Research - Edition: First, 1347 AH.

4- Al-Jahiz (died: 869 AD): *Al Hayawan (the animal)* – Dar Al Kotob Al-Alami- edition: second, 1424 AH.

5- Ibn Qutaiba Al-Dinouri (died: 889 AD): Ayoun Al-Akhbar - Dar Al-Kutub Al-Alami - Publishing Date: 1418 AH.

6- Ibn al-Marzban (died: 921 AD) *Manuscript: The virtue of dogs over many of those who wore clothes* - from the Azhar Library - No. 313459.

7- Al-Tabari (died: 923 AD): *Tarikh al-Omam wa al-Muluk (History of Nations and Kings)* - Dar Al-Kutub Al-Alami - First Edition, 1407 AH.

8- Abu Bakr Al-Khairati (died: 939 AD): *Makarem Al-Akhlak w Maaleha w Mahmoud Taraekha (The Honors and high Morals and Their Best Ways)* – Dar Al Afak Al Arabya - Edition: First, 1419 AH - 1999 AD.

9 - Ibn Abd Rabbu Al-Andalusi (died: 940 AD): *Al Akd Al-Fareed (The Unique Contract)* – Dar Al-Kutub Al-Almi- Edition: First, 1404 AH.

10 - Ibn al-Faqih (died: about 951 AD): *Al-Baladan (countries)* – Alem Al-Kutub- Edition: First, 1416 AH - 1996 AD.

11 - Al-Tnoukhi (died: 994 AD): *Neshwar Al Mohadara and Akhbar Al-Mozakara (lecture session and study news)* - publication year: 1391 AH.

12- Abu Hilal Al-Askari (died: after 1005 AD): *Jamhara Al- Amthal (The People of Proverbs)* - Dar Al-Fikr - Second Edition, 1988.

13- Abu Hayyan Al-Tawhidi (died: about 1010 AD): *Al-Basaer w Al Zakhaer (Insights and Ammunition)* - Dar Sader - Edition: First, 1408 AH - 1988 AD.

14- Miskawayh (died: 1030 AD): *Tagareb Al-Omam w Taakeb Al-Hemam (Experiences of nations and succession of determination)* - Publisher: Sorush - Edition: Second - 2000 AD.

15- Abu Mansour Al-Thaalabi (died: 1038 AD): *Themar Al Kolob fe Al-Modaf w Al-Mansoub* - Dar Al-Maarif.

16- Ibn Rashik Al-Qayrawani (died: 1071AD): *Al-Omda fe Mahasen Al Sher w Adabeh* – Dar-Algel - Edition: Fifth, 1401 AH - 1981 AD.

17- Ibn Abd al-Barr al-Qurtubi (died: 1071 AD): *Bahga Al-Magales w Anas Al-Magales*- Dar Al-Kutub Al-Almi.

18 - Al-Khatib Al-Baghdadi (died: 1072 AD): *Tarekh Baghdad* - Dar Al-Gharb Al-Islami - Edition: First, 1422 AH - 2002 AD.

19- Abu Ubaid al-Bakri (died: 1094 AD): *Al-Masalek w Al-Mamalek* - Dar al-Gharb al-Islami - Publication Year: 1992 AD.

20- Sahari (died: 1117 AD): *Al-Ansab* - Fourth Edition - 1427 AH – 2006 AD.

21- Abu Al-Fadl Ahmad Al-Maydani (died: 1124 AD): *Magmeh Al Amthal* - Dar Al-Marefa

22- Al-Tartushi (died: 1126 AD): *Siraj al-Muluk* - one of the first Arab publications - Egypt - Publication Date: 1289 AH, 1872 AD.

23- Ismail Al-Asbhani (died: 1141 AD): *Ser Al-Salaf Al Salehen (Biography of the Righteous Predecessors)* - Al-Raya Publishing House - First Edition - 1420 AH - 1999 AD.

24- Jarallah al-Zamakhshari (died: 1144 AD): *Al-Mustaqsi in Amthal Al- Arabs* - Dar Al-Kutub Al-Alami - Edition: Second, 1987.

25- *Rabi'a Al-Abrar w Nosos Al-Akhiar* - Al-Alami Foundation - Edition: First, 1412 AH.

26- Al-Samani (died: 1167 AD): Al-Ansab - the Council of the Ottoman Encyclopedia, Hyderabad - edition: first - 1382 AH - 1962 AD.

27 - Ibn Hamdun (died: 1167 AD): *The Hamdouni Tazkara* - Dar Sader - Edition: First - 1417 AH.

28- Ibn Asaker (died: 1176 AD): *Tarekh Demeshk* (History of Damascus) - Dar al-Fikr - 1415 AH - 1995 AD.

29 - Abu Taher Al-Salafi (died: 1180 AD): *Mogem Al-Safar (A Dictionary of Travel)* – AlMaktaba Al-Togariya - Makkah Al-Mukarramah.

30- Ibn al-Jawzi (d. 1201 AD): Al-Montazem fe Tarekh Al-Omam w AlMuluk - Dar Al-Kutub Al-Alami - Edition: First, 1412 AH - 1992 AD.

31- *Ketab Al-Azkya* - Al-Ghazali Library.

32- Ruby of Hamwi (died: 1229 AD): *Mogem Al Boldan (Glossary of Countries)* - Dar Sader - Edition: Second, 1995.

33- *Mogem Al-Odabaa = Ershad Al-Areeb Ela Marefa Al-Adib* - Dar Al-Gharb Al-Islami - Edition: First, 1414 AH - 1993 AD.

34- Izz al-Din Ibn al-Atheer (died: 1233 AD): *Al-Lebab fe Tahzeeb Al-Ansab* - Dar Sader.

35- Sabat Ibn al-Jawzi (died: 1256 AD): *Merah Al-Zaman fe Twarekh Al-Ayan* - Dar al-Resala International - Edition: First, 1434 AH - 2013 AD.

36- Al-Qazwini (died: 1283 AD): *Athar Al-Belad w Akhbar Al-Ebad* - Dar Sader.

37- Ibn Manzur (died: 1311 AD): *Mokhtasar Tarekh Demeshk (A Brief History of Damascus)* by Ibn Asaker - Dar al-Fikr - Edition: First, 1402 AH - 1984 AD.

38- Al-Nuwairi (died: 1333 AD): *Nehayt Al-Erab fe Fonon Al-Adab* - House of Books and National Documents - Edition: First, 1423 AH.

39- Ibn Aybak Al-Dawadari (deceased: after 1336 AD): *Kenz Al-Durar w Gamea Al-Gharr* - Publisher: Issa Al-Babi Al-Halabi - Investigation: Edward Biden, 1414 AH - 1994 AD.

40- Al-Dhahabi (died: 1348 AD): *Tarekh Al-Eslam w Wafiyat Al-*

Mashaheer w Al-Alam – Dar-AlGharb Al-Eslami - Edition: First, 2003 AD.

41- *Ser Alam Al-Nobala* - Al-Resala Foundation - Edition: 3rd -1405 AH / 1985 AD.

42- Shehab A. Lidin Al-Omari (died: 1349 AD): *Masalek al-Absar fe Mamalek Al-Amsar* - Cultural Foundation, Abu Dhabi - Edition: First, 1423 AH.

43- Zain Al-Din Ibn Al-Wardi (died: 1349 AD): *Tarekh Ibn Al-Wardi* – Dar-Al-Kutub Al-Elmiya - Edition: First, 1417 AH - 1996 AD.

44- Salah Al-Din Al-Safadi (died: 1363 AD): *Al-Wafi Belwafiyat* – Dar Ehya Al-Torath - 1420 AH - 2000 AD.

45- Taj al-Din al-Sibki (d. 1370 AD): *Tabakat Al-Shafeya Al-Kobra* - Hajar - Edition: Second, 1413 AH.

46- Ibn Katheer (died: 1373AD): *Al-Bedaya w Al-Nehaya* – Dar Ehyaa Al-Torath Al-Arabi - first edition: 1408 AH - 1988 AD

47- Kamal al-Din al-Damiri (died: 1405 AD): *Hayat Alhaywan Al-Kobra (The Great Animal Life)* – Dar Al-Kutub Al-Elmi - Edition: Second, 1424 AH.

48 - Ibn Khaldun (died: 1406 AD): *Tarekh Ibn Khaldun* - Dar Al-Fikr, Edition: Second, 1408 AH - 1988 AD.

49 – Al-Fayrouz Abad (deceased: 1415AD): *Al-Kamous Al-Moheet* - Al-Resala Foundation - Edition: Eighth, 1426AH-2005AD.

50- Al-Qalqashandi (died: 1418 AD): *Kalaed Al-Jaman feltareef be Qabael Arab al-Zaman* - Dar al-Kitab al-Masri, Dar al-Kitab al-Libani - Edition: second, 1402 AH - 1982 AD.

51- Taqi al-Din al-Maqrizi (died: 1441 AD): *Al-Mawaez w Al-Eatebar Bezekr Al-Khatat w Al-Athar* - Dar Al-Kutub Al-Alami - Edition: First, 1418 AH.

52- Al-Abhishey Abu Al-Fath (d. 1448AD): *The Mustatrif fe Kol Fan Mostatref* – Alam Al-Kutub - Edition: First, 1419 AH.

53- Ibn Hajar Al-Asqalani (died: 1449 AD): *Nozhat Al-Albab fe Al-Alqab*

- Al-Rushd Library - Edition: First, 1409 AH–1989 AD.

54- Abdel Moneim Al-Hamiri (died: 1495 AD): *Al-Rawd Al-Maatar fe Khabar Al-Aktar* - Nasser Foundation for Culture - Edition: Second, 1980 AD.

55- Yusef bin Abd al-Hadi (died: 1503 AD): *Al-Eghterab fe Ahkam Al-Kelab*- Dar Al-Watan - Edition: First 1417 AH.

56- Jalal al-Din al-Suyuti (died: 1505 AD): *Hosn Al-Mohadara fe Tarekh Misr w Al-Qahira* - Dar Al-Ahyaa Al-Arabiya - Edition: First 1387 AH - 1967 AD.

57- *Al-Hawi Lel-Fatwa in Fiqh, Olom Al-Tafseer, Hadith, Osoul, Nahw w Al-Erab w Saer Al-Fonoun* – Dar Al-Kutub Al-Almi - Edition: First - 1421 AH - 2000 AD.

58- Haji Khalifa (died: 1657 AD): *Kashf al-Zonoun An Asami Al-Kutub w Al-Fonoun* - Al-Muthanna Library - Publication Date: 1941 AD.

59- Abd al-Qadir al-Baghdadi (died: 1682 AD): *Khezana Al-Adab W Lob Lebab Lesan Al-Arab* - Al-Khanji Library - Edition: Fourth, 1418 AH - 1997 AD.

60- Abu al-Fida (d. 1715 AD): *Rouh Al-Bayan* - Dar al-Fikr.

61- Al-Zubaidi Muhammad al-Husayni (d. 1790 AD): *Tag Al-Arous* - Dar al-Hidaya.

62- Zainab al-Amiliyyah (died: 1914 AD): *Al Dawrr Al-Manthor fe Tabakat Rabat Al-Khodour* - Al-Amiriya Grand Printing Press, Egypt - Edition: First, 1312 AH.

63- Mustafa Al-Rafei (d. 1937 AD): *Tarekh Adab Al-Arab* - Arab Book House.

64 - Al-Zarkali (died: 1976 AD): *Al-Alam* - Dar Al-Alam for Millions - Edition: Fifteenth - 2002 AD.

65- *Keset Ketab* - Zuhair Zaza - Al-Warraq website.